Born With It:

Unleashing Your Greatness

Born With It:

Unleashing Your Greatness

By

JB Smiley Jr.

ISBN: 978-0-578-18190-5

Contents

Foreword

I have known JB Smiley, Jr. for 8 years. He exemplifies the definition of hard work. When JB and I met in college, one of the first statements he made to me was, "I am a realist." At first, I did not understand what he meant and I assumed it was just Memphis jargon. In fact, I even argued that there is no such thing, but as I became close friends and teammates with JB, I noticed that he was a man of his word. When JB sets his mind to do something, he does everything in his power to see that it comes to fruition.

What I love most about JB, is the message he is sharing with the world: you are "Born With It." As you discover your "It," you will begin to see doors open in your life, you will develop more confidence, establish better discipline, have more energy, and a greater passion for your dreams. Your "It" may not come to you all at once, but I have a sense that as you go through this book, your "It" will become clear.

The book you are holding in your hand is not another self-help book. This book is full of principles, wisdom, and real life practicality that will help you to improve your thought process toward life. Allow the stories and the words in this book to transform how you live your life. Grab your notebook, highlighter, and pen; then, find a coffee shop or a quiet place, because this book is about to rock your world!

With Love,

J. Scott Samarco

Acknowledgements

While growing up, I frequently heard the saying, "It takes a village to raise a child." After writing this book, I can say with confidence that it takes a village to write a book. Throughout this process, I received an immense amount of support from several people, and I would like to briefly acknowledge some, individually.

First, I would like to thank Ms. Dominique King, Esq. While in law school, I would give her a hard time because she would spend so much time on minor details. If I had known that her attention to detail would have continued to be a source of many of my headaches during this book writing process, I would have persuaded her to drop out. But seriously, I could not have done this without her.

Second, I would like to thank Mr. Michael L. Harris, J.D. Mr. Harris' role in my life has frequently changed: boss, advisor, mentor, and friend. His latest role was as my part-time editor; part-time only because he was too busy to be my full-time editor. That is what happens when you are as talented as he is. I am truly grateful for his help.

Third, I would like to thank Mrs. Shari Watt, M.S. We have been friends longer than I can comfortably say without feeling old. Because of our friendship, she felt extremely comfortable correcting me during this process as if I were one of her elementary school students. Thankfully, I am not. She was amazing throughout.

Fourth, I would like to thank Ms. Lacretia Carroll, Ph.D. (c). Admittedly, I do most of my work when the rest of the world is sleeping and more times than I can remember, I called her at very strange hours talking about concepts within this book. Although she fussed at least half of the time, she almost always answered the phone. Her insight is appreciated, her fussing not so much. This would not have been possible without her.

Last but not least, I would like to thank my family, friends, loved ones, and supporters. Their words of encouragement over the past few years have meant so much to me.

Section 1: Discovering Your Inherent Power

"Never underestimate the power of dreams and the influence of the human spirit. We are all the same in this notion: The potential for greatness lives within each of us." – *Wilma Rudolph*

Inherent Power! We all possess it!

Whether you believe in the big bang theory or creationism, there is at least one fact that cannot be disputed regardless of which side of the track you are on — people are born with certain innate abilities and characteristics that make every individual unique. These innate abilities can manifest in a number of ways, from natural orators to natural athletes. These abilities do not guarantee success in any particular field. However, the abilities indicate that we are here for a particular reason, and that particular reason has been illustrated since the beginning of time.

A well-known story taught to students seeking a Master of Divinity is found in the Old Testament of the Bible. The story is about Noah and how God saw something in Noah, which led to God sparing his life as well as his family. In this story, God tells Noah that there will be a great flood. Noah builds an ark to withstand a one hundred and fifty-day flood.[1] During the flood, every human being perished except Noah, his wife, his sons, and

---

[1] Bible, Genesis Chapter 6 – Chapter 7.

their wives.[2] According to the Bible, when the flood water receded, Noah and his family came out of the ark and repopulated the Earth.[3]

Another, but distinct, concept about a selected group surviving can be found in science—Charles Darwin's Theory of Natural Selection. In the interest of brevity, it can be summed up by saying that the stronger and more advanced members of a species flourish and the weaker ones die off. Hence, if you are currently reading this book, regardless of whether you are a Christian or atheist, you are a descendant of a survivor and part of a stronger and more advanced group.

If you think about it, the two concepts can be reconciled; we are fortunate enough to make it this far because we were born with everything essential for us to prosper. Simply put, you are Born With It!

"Born With It" is not your typical motivational book. If you are expecting or wanting that type of book, this is not the book for you. "Born With It" will focus on techniques that will allow you to tap into, utilize, and maximize your inherent power. As such, this book will be divided into three major sections: I. Discovering Your Inherent Power, II. Utilizing Your Inherent Power, and III. Maximizing Your Inherent Power. It is imperative that we do not undervalue the importance of investing in ourselves. Putting the necessary time, money, and energy

---

[2] Bible, Genesis 7:24.

[3] Bible, Genesis 9:1.

into all areas of our lives will be well worth it. The time spent reading this book is a well-placed investment.

Let's be honest, most of us play it safe even when it comes down to investing in ourselves. Nevertheless, we would all like to see more, do more, and accomplish more. But that is easier said than done. The problem for some, like myself, is that they are overly shy, fearful of rejection or failure, unsure of themselves, or full of other insecurities that hinder growth. What these individuals do not know or have yet to discover is their untapped potential for greatness. Others are born with utmost confidence but find it difficult to get over the next hurdle. "Born With It" will help you tap into your potential for greatness. Once you have done so, you will become the best version of yourself. At that point, your drive to accomplish your goals will supplant whatever insecurity or shortcoming you have and get you over that hurdle.

"Born With It" is very straightforward and practical. Whether you are a high school student just trying to find yourself, a public speaker struggling to captivate the audience, a business owner looking to take your business to the next level, an employee trying to become an employer, or a first-time author, there is something in this book for you. What you are looking for may not be at the beginning of the book. As such, this book is written in a way that allows you, the reader, to start reading from the chapter or section that speaks to where you are in your life. However, I do encourage you to read from the beginning because each chapter is its own gem.

Chapter 1
Turning Off the Noise

"Determine who you are and what your brand is, and what you're not. The rest of it is just a lot of noise." – Geoffrey Zakarian

In the aftermath of the 90's gangster rap revolution, mainstream media outlets, lawmakers, politicians, religious organizations, and community activist launched a political campaign to ban the use of offensive lyrics in rap music on the radio. One organization sponsored a petition to the President of the United States, Congress, and the FCC, which stated, "The brain is far more than a think tank. Music and song lyrics do not go in one ear and out the other; out of sight is not out of mind. The brain RECORDS AND STORES everything it sees, hears, tastes, smells, and touches. CYAA [children, youth, and young adults] of the Black nation are involuntarily being programmed to murder by enTRAINment; a proven scientific process by which the brain is enTRAINed to become one with that to which it repetitiously hears, sees, records, and stores."[4] Their essential claim was, we are what we listen to; I see things differently. The world is filled with people, places, and things that could potentially influence us. This does not mean that we are powerless in life. We have within us the ability to focus, think, and reason…and from these powers combined we derive the

---

[4] PETITION THE PRESIDENT/CONGRESS/FCC TO BAN GANGSTA HATE RAP,
https://www.change.org/p/gangsta-rap-is-hate-speech.

supreme power of choice. It is not what we hear that makes or breaks us; it is what we choose to listen to. This chapter is about listening, and learning the difference between influences that are good and bad, helpful and useless, positive and negative, music and "NOISE." Noise is anything in your life that clouds your judgment, distracts, discourages, or hinders you from reaching your full potential or discovering and tapping into your inherent power.

We all encounter noise at some point in our lives; often, it starts before we have any control over the things we see or do. For me, the most challenging and pressing noise I encountered had nothing to do with any of my shortcomings, but everything to do with statistics. According to statistics, individuals who grow up in poverty will likely repeat the cycle. Statistics provide that we are products of our environment. Similarly, statistics show that people who grow up in a non-traditional, dysfunctional, or a single-parent home are likely to fail. To be as blunt and transparent as possible, my parents divorced when I was four years old. Because of this, at various times, I thought that I would be a statistic.

My mother worked two jobs so that I could have the means to experience things she only dreamed of as a child. However, our financial stability came at a price. I was home alone during my teenage years with absolutely no supervision and ample opportunity to become another statistic. As I grew older, I realized that statistics only take into account information that is readily available. Statistics did not take into account that my parents remained friends, that they would remarry years later, or that I possessed the inherent power to overcome, exceed expectations, and blatantly refused to be a statistic.

Although statistics may not be favorable for you, understand that deep inside of you is an inherent power to do more, want more, and achieve more. This inherent power allows you to refuse to be a statistic and overcome any negativity in your life. Like the statistical noise for those of us who are born into certain categories or environments, all noise needs to be turned off. Noise has varying degrees of severity and can come from several different people including friends, family, associates, and even outsiders. An environment itself can also be considered noise. The best place to start muting and/or eliminating noise from our lives is our relationships.

People change and evolve into unique, better versions of themselves. Good working relationships should do the same. The rule is simple. Positive relationships promote growth, development, and strength; negative relationships are unproductive and exhausting. "Noise" is the by-product of negativity, and it lives in drama, doubt, confusion, and unfortunately, in bad relationships. The process of filtering noise from our lives requires us to evaluate our relationships and the things that influence the way we act, think, and respond to what happens in life. In doing so, we gain the information necessary to choose our relationships wisely and limit our exposure to other negative influences.

Human interaction is an important part of life, and for the aspiring, is quintessential to the achievement of success. Human interaction generally leads to the development of relationship connections. These connections come in many forms. Some connections evolve into associate level relationships, while others become more intimate. The most popular connections are the familial relationships we are born into, not to mention friendships and professional relationships. No matter the type of relationship, we must learn to recognize productive relationships and distinguish them from the noisy relationships...then we must place the negative relationships outside our circle of influence. The same must be done to our unproductive habits and behaviors. This will give us the best chance of creating a productive plan for our lives, which whether we like it or not, will have an impact on our family as well. We should be cognizant of the potential consequences the plan for our lives will have, both short term and long term. Family, friends, associates, and outsiders[5] will all weigh in and give their input. Often, this input is unsolicited and usually begins like this: 1) I know what is best for you; 2) I just want you to be happy; 3) You should try doing this; 4) Do not waste your time doing that; or 5) Just listen to me. In addition to the "advice," there are other distractions or noise we hear or have to deal with while formulating our plan. Other noise consists of naysayers and negative environments in general. At some point, you have to turn the noise off.

---

[5] Outsiders in this context means individuals other than family, friends, and associates.

"Turning off the noise" is a task that should be handled with care. You should think before you speak in most situations, but especially when turning off the noise. This is because most solicited and unsolicited "advice" comes from those closest to us. If you act abruptly without thought, it can lead to strained relationships with those you hold dear. As such, you must pay particular attention to these relationships when attempting to turn the noise off.

Associate Noise

An associate is a person who you work or spend time with.[6] It is also defined as one associated with another as a partner, colleague, companion or comrade.[7] Associates are people in your life for a particular reason, usually business related. They have the ability to either assist or sabotage. Thus, "associate noise" is particularly dangerous. The dangerousness of "associate noise" is three-fold: you are usually required to associate with these individuals; they are in a position to have a direct effect on you, whether good or bad; and the noise will not necessarily be obvious, although it can be.

An associate can make your professional life, which includes graduate and undergraduate studies, more difficult. They can spread distasteful rumors or go out their way to make you feel incompetent, which makes your time amongst them a nightmare. Possible examples of

---

[6] Webster's Dictionary.

[7] Webster's Dictionary.

"associate noise" are comments such as, "Maybe you are not cut out for this," or "You might just have too much on your plate to do your job effectively," or "They are not treating you right; if I were you I would quit." If you hear or have heard things like this from an associate, be wary and see if the person is legitimately concerned. If not, what you are hearing or have heard was likely "associate noise." Turn it off!

Family & Friend Noise

This category of noise is almost self-explanatory. You share a unique bond with your family and friends; some you grew up with, and others you allow to be a part of your life. Because of this, they know more about you than anyone else, from your shortcomings to your hang-ups. If you ever need to talk, they are the ones you call and vice versa. The mutual trust is what makes family and friend noise the most dangerous.

"You know I love you," or "I only want the best for you," is likely what will precede family and friend noise. Although those words are likely true, the words that follow may do more harm than good. If what is being said discourages, belittles, or hinders your growth, be skeptical. The fact that someone loves or cares about you does not make him or her an expert in everything about you. You must be cognizant of family and friend noise. It can plant a seed of self-doubt or lead you astray. Hence, turning off family & friend noise is essential to your progress.

Negative Noise

Negative noise is more general than the other categories of noise. It is essentially the catchall category. It includes places and people that allow negativity to fester and flourish. Negative noise is distinguishable from the other types of noise because for the most part, excluding a selected few environments, the people and places included are usually not beneficial in any shape, form, or fashion. Hence, most of the naysayers and pessimists in your life fall into this category. Negative noise, unlike associate or family and friend noise, is easy to spot. Let me flush this out a bit more.

Environments that allow negativity to flourish are detrimental to anyone subjected to it. This could be a number of places, from your current place of employment to the place you consider home. It should be noted that if the negative noise is coming from the home, refer back to the family and friend noise section for for further guidance. In regards to naysayers and pessimists, also known as haters, they are the individuals that speak against any goals you have set for yourself or generally doubt your ability. Being around negative noise is physically, mentally, and emotionally draining. Avoid it if at all possible.

After discussing the different types of noise, one question remains: "How do you turn off the noise?" It's quite simple; well, that is not entirely true, but the process has been simplified into a three step process, which I have coined the four D's: diligently listen, due consideration or dismiss, then directly address.

The Four D's

Diligently listen. When I was a middle-schooler, I had the habit of saying "I hear you" whenever someone was attempting to correct me, especially my teachers. I heard what was being said, but I effectively tuned them out. I was not diligently listening. Apparently, at that age, I did not understand that hearing what's being said is not sufficient, nor is it equivalent to diligently listening. But what exactly is diligently listening?

The concept can be better explained by a story about former IBM CEO Sam Palmisano's trip abroad. Mr. Palmisano was up against a language barrier after being assigned to lead IBM Japan.[8] While there, he stated that he learned to listen.[9] He said "I learned to listen by having only one objective: comprehension. I was only trying to understand what the person was trying to convey to me. I wasn't listening to critique or object or convince."[10] Mr. Palmisano's approach to listening is a stark contrast to my "I hear you" approach of my middle school days. Mr. Palmisano was diligently listening.

---

[8] Aimee Groth, *Sam Palmisano Learned This Leadership Lesson While Doing Business In Japan* available at http://www.businessinsider.com/what-sam-palmisano-learned-in-japan-2012-4; Don Sturgill, *Learn How to Listen Better – And Win More Customers* available at http://conversionmax.com/listening-skills/

[9] *Id.*

[10] *Id.*

Diligently listening is paying attention with the sole purpose of understanding the message the person speaking is attempting to convey. Step 1, diligently listening, will require you to listen for comprehension. This step is essential to the process because it cannot be determined whether something is noise without listening to it first. Diligently listening will put you in the best position to make that determination. Open your ears and mind, then listen.

Consider this following hypothetical. Marcus has been working at his current place of employment for two years. During that time, he began to associate with Josh, his co-worker. Josh has repeatedly told him that he should seek other employment and has even provided him with a list of potential jobs. In this scenario, Marcus should first diligently listen to Josh.

***Due consideration* or *dismiss*.** This is a vital step; it is where you decide either to take heed to the advice given or disregard it and consider it noise. Whichever decision you make can and probably will have a lasting effect. Black's Law Dictionary defines due consideration as the degree of attention properly paid to something, as the circumstances merit.[11] Due consideration is only given when what you are hearing is beneficial; noise is the furthest thing from it.

Dismiss is defined as treating something as unworthy of serious consideration, or deliberately ceasing to think about it. If what you are hearing is not beneficial,

---

[11] Black's Law Dictionary 9th Edition (p. 574).

dismiss it and consider it noise. This is something I learned over time.

In my second year of law school, I vividly remember having to decide due consideration or dismiss. I felt as if I proved myself as a competent legal scholar and orator. I developed what I believed to be a rapport with most of my colleagues. There seemed to be a mutual respect amongst us, so I thought. Then, Rose happened.

During my second year of law school, I was offered a summer associate position[12] at Rose Law Firm, which will forever be connected with Hillary Clinton,[13] although I did not take part in on-campus interviews like some of my colleagues. After being offered the position, I returned to class the following week. During that week and the week thereafter, I thought things were fine as usual, but something was not quite right. I was made aware that some of my colleagues were questioning my qualifications for the position. Some of the things that were said or directed my way were extremely hurtful. "Is he Rose Law Firm material?" "Is he even smart enough?" "They just needed to hire a minority." "He better thank God for affirmative action." Initially, after being made aware of the comments, I walked around with a chip on my shoulder. I

---

[12] A Summer Associate position is essentially a law clerk for the summer. A law clerk is an individual, usually a current law student, who provides assistance to the lawyer or law firm in which he or she works. The law clerk performs various task such as drafting legal memorandum and legal research while getting on the job training.

[13] Hillary Clinton was an attorney at Rose Law Firm during her time in Little Rock, AR.

wanted to know every single person who had something negative to say. I went from smiling throughout the day to a cold stare whenever I believed I was in the presence of someone who took part in the negative banter. The noise was beginning to control my emotions and my ability to reason. One of my colleagues, who later became a friend, took notice. She asked me, "Why are you so concerned with what was said?" When I began to think about her question, I did not have a legitimate reason. What they thought about me had no bearing on my life or future aspirations. At that point, I had two options: continue giving due consideration or dismiss. I chose to dismiss!

Daily, we are presented with information about us or the goals we may have from various individuals, and we all must face that very same question, due consideration or dismiss?

If after diligently listening, you choose to give due consideration to the information presented to you, be sure to assign it the appropriate weight. Some things should be taken with a grain of salt, which means to maintain some degree of skepticism. It is usually apparent how much weight you should give to the information or advice being directed your way. However, sometimes this is simply not true.

Growing up, I was fortunate to have genuine friends in elementary, middle, and high school whom truly cared for me and my well-being. They wanted to see me succeed. Because of the friends I had earlier on, I grew accustomed to completely trusting anyone who held themselves out as my friend. However, my trend of making true friends did not carry over to undergrad. My first year of college, I quickly became acquainted with several people. I drew closer to one particular person because we had similar backgrounds — same high school, athletes, good students, and similar taste in women. In my mind at the time, this was the formula for a solid friendship. In the words of the great Kevin Hart, "You gone learn today!" I sure did.

During our "friendship," I would discuss some of my personal issues with him. He would give sound advice about everything — in hindsight every area except for one. I did not notice he was intentionally trying to sabotage one area of my life. I gave due consideration to everything he said because he had given me nothing but good advice in the other areas of my life. On several occasions, my girlfriend would call, and he would say things like, "She must not trust you because she always calls when you are out." That slowly became "I would not put up with that if I were you." Needless to say after causing me to have doubts about my relationship, my girlfriend and I broke up. Shortly after that, he was attempting to converse with her on a more intimate level.

In retrospect, it was apparent that I should have maintained some degree of skepticism. The fact that he seemed sincere, gave sound advice in the past, and held himself out as my friend, clouded my judgment. Do not make that mistake! Diligently listen to everything directed your way, and if you choose to give due consideration, assign an appropriate weight based on the merit of what is being said.

Picking back up with our hypothetical about Marcus and Josh, Marcus was preparing to listen diligently to Josh. After listening, Marcus determined that Josh had a valid reason for offering the advice. Josh legitimately believed that Marcus was overqualified for his current position. Josh had learned that Marcus recently graduated with a master's degree in business management. It appeared Josh's reasons for providing the list of jobs were legitimate. Marcus decided to give due consideration to the message Josh was conveying. When determining how much weight he would give to Josh's advice, Marcus made a mental note of a few things: the other jobs offered better salaries, the other jobs would give him the opportunity to work in his degree field, and that Josh would be the person next in line for Marcus' current position if he were to leave. Marcus' next step is to directly address.

Directly address. There are times when being passive serves a purpose, and it proves beneficial. This is not one of those times; directly addressing the issue is a must. If you allow the noise in your life to continue unaddressed, it can consume you. After you have determined that the advice presented to you is noise, you should keep in mind that a family or friend likely means well. As I stated previously, you should tailor your response to the particular situation or person. Nevertheless, be assertive but careful not to be disrespectful. Communicate your comments, concerns, and criticism. Clearly state why the information presented to you clouds your judgment, distracts, discourages, or hinders you from reaching your full potential. Directly addressing the situation in such a manner will likely lead to good results, especially when the individual on the receiving end is someone who cares—family or friends.

It should be noted that addressing this in an inappropriate manner could lead to a severed relationship and cause a once friendly environment to become hostile. Be mindful of this when addressing your concerns. What I have found to be beneficial when directly addressing family and friend or associate noise is dealing with the person in private. When done in a public setting, egos and pride usually serve as an impediment to reaching a resolution.

When we last left Marcus and Josh, Marcus made a mental note of the reasons Josh was informing him about other job opportunities. Marcus knew that he had to address Josh directly. The next day, when the two crossed paths, Marcus discreetly asked to speak to Josh in private. Later that day, Josh came by Marcus' office. Marcus stated that he had given due consideration to Josh's advice. Marcus further explained he knew that Josh was next in line for his job if he chose to leave; however, he did feel that applying for the other jobs would be in his best interest. Marcus assured Josh that if he decided to leave, he would do what he could to make sure that Josh gets his current job. The two shook hands and parted ways. It should be noted that if Marcus chose to dismiss the advice, he would have directly addressed Josh in the same manner.

The sad truth is, noise is an unavoidable part of life. Your response to it often determines the outcome. The three step approach—diligently listen, due consideration or dismiss, and directly address—gives you the tools needed to appropriately address the noise in your life. However, some noise cannot be turned off, even after applying the three-step approach. At this point, you can attempt to tune out the noise or use it to fuel your personal drive to succeed.

Growing up you were probably taught the following rhyme at some point in grade school, "Sticks and stones may break my bones, but words will never hurt me." You were essentially being taught or conditioned to tune out the noise. The saying you were taught to remember in your youth says words will never hurt, but when the noise is extremely severe or communicated repeatedly, it can take a toll on you mentally. To that extent, it is likely to have damaging effects. Tuning out the noise is most effective when the noise is only communicated infrequently, once or twice.

But if the noise is spoken consistently, it may prove difficult to tune out. Realistically, there is only so much a person can take or tune out. If tuning out the noise is ineffective, and the noise begins to dominate your thoughts, convert those negative thoughts into positive energy. Use the noise as fuel to your personal drive to succeed. Consider it as motivation. There will be a point in your life when you will need to do so. For me, it happened to be my last year of undergraduate studies.

My senior year in college, one of my professors would make comments not becoming of someone of that status. The professor had the habit of downplaying the intellectual capacity of male athletes. Naturally, I took opposition to my professor's comments, but I kept my peace. I attempted to tune out the comments my professor made. As the year went on, the comments continued. I told myself that the comments did not affect my grade, I would be graduating soon, and there was little need to address my professor. Boy, was I wrong!

During the last few weeks of class, just before graduation, we had a take home final in the professor's class. I spent hours reading, answering, doing additional reading, and revising before I turned in my final. Unbeknownst to me, my final grade was posted prior to me turning in my final. I received a "C" in the course—a "C" I did not deserve. Initially, I was not going to fight it, but then I realized that I received a "C" in every course the professor taught.

Immediately, I called my professor and inquired about my grade being posted prior to the final being turned in. The professor rudely responded by saying that I did not deserve a better grade, and if I wanted one I better talk to a professor who caters to athletes. My professor's next statements have motivated me ever since. My professor indicated that reading my work was not necessary because I, like all other male athletes, was not capable or deserving of anything other than a "C." My professor continued and said that I have been given things my entire life because I was an athlete, and like most athletes, I will not amount to anything. I realized at that moment I could no longer tune out the noise.

I had to wait until after graduation before I could begin the appeal process. I was patient and used the time before I could start the appeals process to gather all of my work from professor's classes. I not only intended to appeal the one class, but all of the grades I received in the professor's classes. When the appeals process began, I had just moved back to Memphis, Tennessee. I complied with every step of the process. The last step was to come and meet with the appeals board and my professor face-to-face. I relished the opportunity. However, there was a catch; Memphis was over five hundred miles away from my undergraduate institution. They assumed I would not show.

The day before the hearing, I gathered all of my documents, completed work assignments, email exchanges between my professor and I, and hit the road toward my undergraduate institution. The morning of the hearing, although I was not big on wearing business clothes at that point of my life, I was appropriately dressed for the occasion. I walked into the hearing and quickly noticed that my professor was nowhere to be found. After an hour-long informal hearing with the appeals committee, I was informed that I would receive an "A" in all three of my professor's classes. Victory! This victory was on a small scale; I was thinking much larger.

My professor's negative comments stuck with me and fueled my desire to succeed in law school as well. Right after I received my law school graduation invitations, I sat one to the side; it was going directly to my professor. By sending the invitation, I was telling my professor off in the most professional way possible. I also included the following note, "The next time you encounter someone in your personal or professional capacity, do not pass judgment. Instead, encourage and support their goals." This is the victory I wanted. I owe some of my success in law school partially to the noise my professor spewed, which fueled my fire and drive to succeed.

Noise will come at you from all angles and directions. It will come from people you hold in high regard and possibly from people you do not know. It will come in the form of a place you must frequent or a place you like to visit. Just know that noise is present and will come, but that is not the end. You have the tools needed to turn off the noise. You can apply the four D's: diligently listen, due consideration or dismiss, then directly address. If you apply this approach to no avail, you can attempt to tune out the noise, but if that does not work, use the noise as a catalyst to take your motivation and drive to the next level. Turning off the noise puts you in a position to succeed; after you have done so, look in the mirror!

Chapter 2
Look in the Mirror

*More important than how we see the world, is how we see
ourselves. Success in life is heavily dependent upon how we
define who we are. - Unknown*

Now that noise is no longer a problem, you are in
perfect position to look in the mirror. In 1835, German
Chemist Justus Von Liebig revolutionized homes all across
the world when he created the modern silver glass
mirror.[14] I'm not sure what sparked Liebig's obsession
with the mirror. He could have been inspired by the pure
science of reflection, but maybe there was more to it. I
believe Liebig was captivated by the irony of the mirror.
The mirror is so simple, yet extraordinarily complex.
People love the mirror and the wonderful sense of
affirmation it gives, and in the same breath, fear the
honesty and unfettered truth of its reflection. The mirror,
for some, is the birthplace of confidence, and for others,
the reminder of flaws. Self-empowerment always begins
with an honest look in the mirror, but not the one hanging
on the wall. The mirror we must gaze deeply into is the
mirror of introspection and self-reflection. We must
honestly embrace what we see and be willing to embrace
all that is good about us, and of course have enough
courage to be truthful.

---

[14] Mr. Liebig developed a process for applying a thin
layer of metallic silver to one side of a pane of glass.

Before we dive into this concept, I literally want you to look in a mirror. I will wait...what did you see? Did you dwell on your imperfections or were you focused on your more appealing attributes? Were you proud of the person looking back at you? Be honest with yourself.

Be Honest With Yourself

Self-examination can help you to understand your greatest strengths and weaknesses if you are honest about what you see. If you are not honest with yourself, you will invest time and sweat equity in areas not meant for you. Have you ever met someone who wants to be a professional singer, but sounds absolutely awful? Or someone seeking to become a rap artist, but lacks the rhythm or the lyrical content? How about someone who dreams of playing professional sports, but is as uncoordinated as they come? Or, what about the person who wants to be a writer, but hates to read? How about the person who intends to be a doctor, but is not interested in science? Honesty is the only tool we have to avoid this kind of fruitless pursuit. Being honest with yourself is all about self-examination. Self-examination is best achieved when we take an honest look in the mirror.

Self-examination *begins* when you look at yourself objectively and identify your strengths, weaknesses, values, and beliefs. The goal is to find the gifts, talents, and attributes that make you unique. This process is all about asking questions and answering them honestly. When you begin this process, your questions should include some of the following: What are my likes and dislikes? What do I enjoy doing the most? What are my mental strengths and weaknesses? What are my physical strengths and weaknesses? Do I prefer to work as a member of a team, or do I prefer individual projects? What are my financial goals? What comes naturally to me? In what areas do I excel? What are my core values? How confident am I in my abilities? Do I have a humble attitude? Am I an optimist, pessimist, or a realist? How is my work ethic? Do I manage my time well? Am I more likely to arrive late, or on time? What makes me unique? What reputation have I established in my career field? If I have a poor reputation, how can I make it better? What are my goals? How can I achieve them? What has been holding me back from pursuing my goals? How can I overcome the obstacle(s)? Do I have enough education to pursue my goals? How can I be better?

These are not the only questions you should ask yourself, but it's a good start. Being honest when answering these questions will give you the information you need to become self-aware and proactive in the pursuit of your dreams. For most of us, we begin this process when something takes place or happens in our lives that we categorize as negative. These events or experiences include heartbreaks, break-ups, getting fired from a job, being single "for too long," failing an exam, or realizing that you are not where you want to be. We also begin this process when we notice some of the same things happening to those around us. In an attempt to avoid those occurrences in our life, we start to self-examine.

Like everything that is discussed within the covers of this book, the ability to self-examine is innate. You have been conducting self-examinations to some degree since your days as a toddler. Think about it...when children are learning to walk, they hold on to everything during the preliminary stages. Children know that they are not physically capable of walking without falling. The only way a child, an adolescent, or an adult can know what he or she is capable of doing is by self-examination.

The first time I remember conducting any type of self-examination was in 1992, when I was only a kindergartener. I attended Fairley Elementary in Memphis, Tennessee. Fairley was located in inner city Memphis, in a neighborhood named Whitehaven, but coined "Blackhaven" by the residents. Like most students my age, I was anxious to go to class. After all, I got to be around other kids, nap, go to recess, and talk with so many other students; according to my mother, it was my favorite part about going to school. Not only did I have fun at school, but I also learned the material at a rapid pace. I would finish my assignments before most of the other students and then begin to disrupt the class by talking too much. My teacher would call my mother and report how wonderful I was doing academically but tell her my conduct was horrible. My mother attempted to get my conduct in check, but she did not have to worry about my grades.

During this time in my life, I would spend much of my free time outside of school with my father's side of the family, the Smileys. In addition to spending most of my time with the Smileys, my father would always talk about the accomplishments of his brothers, sisters, and cousins. All I heard was how great it was to be a Smiley. As expected, my father also attributed my academic achievements to his side of the family. Sometime after my parents divorced and my graduation from kindergarten, we moved to the other side of the city, East Memphis.

As summer vacation was approaching its end, I grew eager to begin first grade at my new school—Ross Elementary—which was a county school at the time. According to the teachers at the school, the students there were learning at a faster pace than the students in the Memphis City Schools, i.e. Fairley Elementary. My mother did not worry because I had been excelling at Fairley. After the first week of class, my teacher sent a note home to inform my mother of my struggles to catch on to the material. My mother told the teacher that I just needed time to adjust to the new environment, and once I made a few friends, I would be fine. My mother truly believed this.

During the next couple of weeks, I managed to make friends, but my grades were still not up to par. At the end of the third week, my teacher sent another note home with me, but this time, it requested a parent-teacher conference. During the conference, my teacher told my mother that my struggles continued. She indicated that she was not sure if it was because the city schools were teaching at a slower pace, or if my struggles had more to do with an inability to comprehend. My mother assured her that any difficulty I had was only temporary. Despite my mother's assurance, she told her it would be best for me to begin attending K-1 if I did not improve. She said K-1 would teach me all the principles I needed to be successful next year when I would begin the first grade for the second time. My mother said okay, and left the conference devastated; this was before she had to tell her baby boy that he might be sent to a kindergarten–like class.

What happened next, I remember vividly. My mother called me into the dining room and told me to have a seat at the kitchen table because we needed to talk. As I approached the kitchen table, I noticed a look of sorrow in her eyes. When we were both seated, she took my hand and told me it was going to be all right, but she had some "not so good" news for me. As engaged as I had ever been, I waited for her to tell me what was going on. I will never forget the next words out of my mother's mouth. "If your grades do not improve soon, you will be placed in K-1." My mother's next statements, which was really a parenting moment, still seem to be a little unorthodox after all these years. She told me if I worked hard and improved my grades by the end of the first six weeks, I could remain in the first grade. She told me in addition to my school work, homework, and school hours, I would have to do work with her at least two hours after school every day, complete all the assignments she assigned from the workbooks she purchased, and dedicate at least 4 hours to studying on the weekend. She said she would not force me to do any of those, but I had to make a decision about what I wanted to do.

That was the moment I recall self-examining, and I was not quite six years old. It felt like time had frozen. My first thought was, "Man! I gotta do all this work!" I started to think about everything that made me unique. Although doubt crept in, I realized that I had to improve not only my weaknesses but also my strengths. Before I knew it, I blurted out, while my mother was sitting there patiently waiting for me to decide, "I can do it! I'm a Smiley!" Although I was extremely young at the time, the uncertainty I experienced at that moment in my life taught me a lifelong lesson — the importance of self-examination.

I would be doing you a disservice if I allow you to believe that the best time or the only time to begin self-examination is after adversity rears its head. You should not wait until you are going through what you perceive to be a negative experience to self-examine. Self-examination should occur when your life is going according to plan, and you do not anticipate any missteps. Self-examination should be proactive. Once you begin the self-examination process, you will gradually become self-aware.

Becoming Self-Aware

I quickly learned over the next couple of weeks, while working to remain in the first grade, that thinking about what made me unique was not enough. It was not sufficient just to be a Smiley. Looking back, it was apparent I did not fully understand my thought processes, but it is obvious to me that I was becoming self-aware.

Before I go too in-depth with the concept of becoming self-aware, let me explain my approach to self-awareness. It begins with two individualized sections—"A closer look" and "Separation."

A closer look. This is the analytical part of self-awareness. Here, you take a closer look at each of your characteristics and attributes you identified while self-examining, and determine whether it is a strength or weakness, whether it is beneficial or detrimental. This determination should be made subjectively and objectively.

No one knows you better than you know yourself. If you are honest with yourself, you will be able to identify most of your strengths and weaknesses. I say most because you will not be able to identify all in either category for one reason or another, whether it is because you are in denial, think too highly of yourself, lack self-confidence or a simple mistake when making the determination; hence, the need for the objective component.

First, think about what areas in your personal and professional life are going well. Next, identify those attributes and characteristics that were essential to getting you there. These attributes and characteristics are usually your strengths. Then, think about those areas in your personal and professional life that appear to be stagnant or in a less than ideal state. Finally, identify those attributes and characteristics that negatively affected or that were responsible for such. These attributes and characteristics are likely your weaknesses. Now, consider asking those individuals that know you best what they perceive to be your strengths and weaknesses. Take note of what is being said.

After you have finished with both the subjective and objective[15] portions of your analytical approach, compare and contrast the strengths and weaknesses identified in the subjective portion with those from the objective portion. The strengths and weaknesses that overlap can almost definitively be said to be your strengths and weaknesses. However, those attributes and characteristics that do not overlap at all may not be an accurate representation of who you are and what you are made of.

Separation. Now it is time for you to put your strengths and weaknesses into separate categories. This will allow you to better assess the areas in your life that need the most attention. Do not fool yourself; no matter how successful you currently are, there are some areas in your life that need improving. That improvement begins by enhancing the characteristics and attributes that make up your strengths and weaknesses.

If I wanted to remain in the first grade, I had to address my weaknesses.

After making a commitment to myself and my mother that I would be willing to do what it takes to improve academically, I had to be honest with myself; I had a lot to work on. This was evidenced by the progress report that accompanied the note from my first-grade teacher requesting a parent-teacher conference. The progress report indicated that I could not differentiate vowel sounds from consonant sounds. It further indicated

---

[15] Objective in this context means asking someone other than yourself.

the way I was taught to write in the city schools was not how it was being taught in the county. Essentially, during the parent-teacher conference, my first-grade teacher told my mother that she believed I was ill prepared for first-grade in a county school.

My mother did not waste any time after I told her I was willing to do what it takes to remain in the first grade; she went to a local bookstore and bought several workbooks to help me improve along with the corresponding teaching materials. Before we got started the next day with what I will call "Mom's School," she asked me what areas I believed I needed to work on. She told me to think about it and tell her prior to Mom's School the next day. It was Friday, and I retired to my room earlier than normal—maybe because I had a lot on my mind or I wanted to start with Mom's School early so that I could play basketball with my friends later. You guess which one. Nevertheless, I still had to answer my mother's question. This was tough for me because I was only five (going on six as I would often tell people who would ask) and had the worst attention span ever. As one of my teachers would always say, "There is no excuse, it is time to produce." Producing is exactly what I did. I am sure she would be proud.

I shut my door, something my father despised when he would visit, and I started going over some of the things I learned in class to figure out my strengths and weaknesses. I quickly realized that my ability to stay on task was not my strong suit. Before I knew it, I began playing my video game. After I had played for thirty minutes or so, I picked back up where I left off. I attempted to go over my consonant sounds, and my vowel sounds to see if I truly was struggling in that area. I remember thinking, "My teacher was not telling the truth." I did the same with my handwriting, but this time, my teacher was definitely on to something. I simply did not know how to write the way the county schools expected.

Early the next morning, I woke up to the smell of pancakes, which is my favorite breakfast food. I rushed into the kitchen and grabbed a plate thinking I was about to get a plateful of delicious pancakes. Before I could fill up my plate with pancakes, my mother told me to come here. She said I had to write down those things I felt like I needed to work on. I grabbed the pencil and paper she had waiting for me and wrote everything I could think of down. I am happy she was not concerned about my spelling, or I would have been there all day. I listed a few things under "bad stuff" and several things under "good stuff." My mother smirked, and I proceeded back to the kitchen where the pancakes were calling my name.

After I had finished eating, it was time for my first day of Mom's School. The first workbook she handed me was a book about improving reading comprehension. She told me to read the story and answer the questions below. I said, "But momma, I already know how to do this." She responded, "Boy you better do what I say." At that moment, I knew Mom's School was serious business. As directed, I began reading. We did the same for every subject matter discussed during regular school regardless if I had identified it in my "bad stuff" category or not. My mother was showing me every area could use some work, even the areas I understood well.

After the first week of Mom's School, I knew what to expect. I came home every day prepared to get to work. The thing about Mom's School is, it did not have a definite start time. Some days my mother was exhausted and would rest after work before we would begin. Others, she would start as soon as she walked through the door from work. At the end of each week, I had a comprehensive test on each subject. I improved quicker than my mother, or I could have imagined. We were not the only ones to take notice of my dramatic improvements.

My first-grade teacher began complimenting me how well I was doing almost immediately after I started Mom's School. When I received my first progress report after week one of Mom's School, it indicated I made all A's for the week. It was a proud moment for my mother and I, but we continued to work as hard as we did when my weaknesses were many. We decided to be proactive so that I would never be in this position again. As I mastered one concept, I moved to the next. This continued even after I was well ahead of my first-grade class.

During Mom's School, I would frequently mention that my birthday was approaching. I may have asked for material gifts, but nothing could compare to the primary gift I sought—a good report card so that I could stay in the first grade. I also wanted to show my father I was just like all the other Smileys he talked about; I wanted to show him that I was smart too. I knew my grades were much better, but I was still uncertain. I turned six on September

8th. A few weeks after my birthday, I received one of the best birthday gifts to date — a report card with all A's and a notification that it was no longer recommended I be placed in K-1.

Self-Aware

Self-awareness is knowing thyself, and being confident in who you are. As you might expect, self-awareness is also knowing who you are not. Being self-aware is absolutely essential when you are attempting to walk in your purpose. In this context, walking in your purpose means, utilizing your gifts, talents, attributes, strengths, and weaknesses (if you have not figured it out by now, this is your inherent power) in the most effective way possible. You can only effectively utilize your inherent power when you are self-aware.

Self-awareness should lead to sound decisions, less emotional responses, choosing a career that fits your abilities, associating with people who bring out the best in you, taking control of your life, knowing what you want, focusing on what you want, and being determined to achieve it. When you become self-aware, you will better understand your actions and reactions, thought processes, and yourself in general. You will no longer have difficulty making the needed changes in your life. Self-awareness puts you in the driver seat of your life, and in turn, you will feel comfortable choosing what you do, how you do it, and the people you allow to be a part of it all.

Before I truly became self-aware, I frequently found myself in situations that did not reflect my values, beliefs, or the principles I held dear. Essentially, the situations were contrary to who I was at the core. These predicaments became more prevalent during my senior year of high school. If I did not become confident in who I was and who I was not, there was no doubt I would end up in prison.

One Friday, I picked up a friend at her home, and like most high school students, my friend and I were looking to get out of the house and have fun for the day. Shortly after picking up my friend, I received a phone call from one of my teammates. He told me that he was at his friend's house, and I should come by. Of course, I obliged. As we were leaving Cordova, my friend asked me where we going, and I told her I was stopping by to see one of my teammates. She responded, "Cool."

As we approached our destination, I realized that we were in my old stomping ground, East Memphis. I practically grew up down the street from our destination and frequented the area. In my mind, I had nothing to worry about; I became less observant than normal. We pulled into the driveway right after nightfall. Because I did not know the owner of the home, I expected my teammate to be outside to greet us. However, his friend was standing outside on the phone.

When I opened my car door and asked him to tell my teammate that I was outside, I realized I had met him previously at a few of our basketball games. He called for my teammate, and my teammate immediately came outside to greet my friend and I. He told us to come into the house and chill with them for a bit. I thought to myself;

anything was better than sitting at home doing nothing, so I agreed. Before I had an opportunity to ask my friend what she wanted to do, my teammate's friend had already engaged her in conversation. I wanted to tell her to follow me, but I knew she would respond by saying, "Do not be a player hater." Instead, I told her I would be right back.

When I entered the house, I realized there were others there as well. I greeted everyone and sat down on the couch near the television. I was so consumed with attempting to seem cool I did not see what was on the table nor did I realize what was taking place. After making myself known and discovering all of the guys knew of me because of basketball, I became more comfortable and observant. Directly in front of me, was a table covered in marijuana. That's not all, surrounding the marijuana was at least two handguns. I say at least two because, at this point, I was in a slight panic, and I was not sure of anything other than what I would look like in stripes.

Although I was sure the police would kick in the door at any moment, I still had time to have an internal debate. Part of me wanted to get up as fast as possible and sprint to my car and never look back, and the other part of me wanted to play it cool and wait until the right moment before I made my exit. I chose the latter. After a minute or so went by, a few of the guys began to bag the marijuana while the other guy loaded the handguns. I attempted to play it cool, but in my mind I was a nervous wreck. I could not help but think, what in the world was going on and how stupid could I be to get myself into this situation. I just knew the only basketball I would be playing would be in the prison yard. I would never have the opportunity to live out my dreams.

I could not wait any longer; I had to leave. At this point, I was not as worried about my reputation for being the cool basketball player as I was about my future. So I did what any person who was scared for their life would do, I exaggerated truth. I stood up and told the guys I had to go because my friend was in the car waiting, we had something to do, and we only had a few more hours before her curfew. The guys told me to go handle that. I promptly exited. What lasted only five minutes seemed like a lifetime.

I realized during those five minutes that I was not about "that life," and if I were to put myself in that situation again, I would probably have a heart attack. I truly understood that self-awareness consisted of more than knowing my strengths and weaknesses, but it also included knowing my purpose, passion, and knowing what I was not. Despite my life flashing before my eyes, that situation helped me become self-aware.

Self-awareness allows you to look in the mirror and see yourself for who you truly are. You will not only be able to identify your gifts, talents, attributes, strengths, and weaknesses, but you will also realize that most of them are innate. Thus, you are born with them. For example, mental toughness, determination, and belief in thyself are all innate attributes.

Think about it. I was only five years old when I told my mother that I could overcome my predicament by working harder than I had before. I had no real understanding of the school system or how anything worked at that point in my life. I thought that my first-grade teacher had the authority to make the determination about my grade placement. Later, I found out my teacher could only recommend placement, but it was ultimately up to my parents if I would be removed from the first grade.

Moreover, I had to show my resolve and mental toughness before I even knew those words existed. We are born with it! I had to be determined to accomplish my goals before I knew how to spell determination. We are born with it! I had to believe that I could achieve before I could read any book that could tell me about the importance of self-belief. More evidence that we are born with it! The "we" is intentional because I am not alone. You too are born with everything you need to achieve your goals. Unleash your greatness!

However, your gifts, attributes, or innate abilities do not come fully developed. Development is a process that usually requires an intentional act to get it jumpstarted.

Section 2: Utilizing Your Inherent Power

On the night of February 05, 2008, a United States Senator from Illinois stood before a very enthusiastic crowd. The crowd chanted and applauded. He smiled and gazed into the crowd and said, "Thank you." The Senator then stated:

> We can do this. We can do this. But it will not be easy. It will require struggle, and it will require sacrifice. There will be setbacks, and we will make mistakes. And that is why we need all the help we can get. So tonight, I want to speak directly to all those Americans who have yet to join this movement but still hunger for change. They know in their gut. They know we can do better than we're doing now… You see, the challenges we face will not be solved with one meeting in one night… Change will not come if we wait for some other person or if we wait for some other time. We are the ones we've been waiting for. We are the change we seek.[16]

When the Senator finished speaking, all that could be heard was the packed crowd chanting, "Yes we can!" This slogan helped a United States Senator in his first term

---

[16] Barack Obama's Feb. 5 Speech, *New York Times*, http://www.nytimes.com/2008/02/05/us/politics/05text-obama.html?_r=0.

become the 44th President of the United States. President Barack Obama's speech and slogan will be forever remembered because it motivated millions and encouraged countless more. Regardless of how you feel about President Obama, he was right. Yes we can!

We can accomplish anything we set out to achieve. However, there will be roadblocks, valleys, mountains, and a litany of other obstacles in our way. To be completely honest, there will be setbacks, and you will make mistakes. It is a part of the growing pains we all must endure. There is a song that says "[t]he race is not given to the swift, nor to the strong, but to the one that endures until the end."[17] But what does it mean to really endure? In order to endure, you have to experience or undergo a hardship. Each and every one of us will have to endure one way or another. You cannot endure unless you are mentally tough. What's remarkable about mental toughness is that the attribute itself is innate, and we all possess it.

Mental toughness alone does not get you where you need to be, but it does put you in the position to take control of your life. At some point, you will have to do so. During childhood, our parents, guardians, and teachers control most aspects of our lives. They make decisions regarding clothing, healthcare, dietary restrictions, schooling, religion, political affiliation, and who we can or cannot associate with. Oftentimes, these decisions are made without consulting us and rightfully so. Not only do they make decisions for us, but also they are usually held

---

[17] For the Good of them by Reverend Milton Brunson.

accountable for any of our shortcomings. When we get older, we have to make those same decisions for ourselves.

But sometimes our love ones or those responsible for us during our childhood become enablers. They allow us to rely on them longer than we should. By enabling us, they are setting us up for failure. There are also circumstances in which those same people who led us through childhood continue to control our lives although we have expressed our intention to control it ourselves. This is usually done by manipulation or when we are financially dependent. However, mental toughness will prepare you to take control of your life. Taking control also includes not making excuses. George Washington Carver once said, "Ninety-nine percent of failures come from people who have the habit of making excuses." Do not allow yourself to become part of this statistic. Stop making excuses and take responsibility for the things that happen in your life, and when you do cease control, you will be more empowered than ever before. You will know you are resilient, intelligent, and stronger than you could have imagined.

There is no room or time for self-doubt. You have something to offer this world. But first, you have to tap into your mental toughness, and when it is time, you must take control and responsibility for your life. The world is waiting!

Chapter 3

Mental Toughness

"Mental Toughness is essential to success." – Vince Lombardi

After turning off the noise and taking a long look in the mirror, you are right where you need to be. You know your strengths and weaknesses. More importantly, you understand that your most valuable assets are innate. Now it is time for you to utilize all facets of your inherent power including mental toughness. This facet of your inherent power must be properly developed. For most, the development of mental toughness begins during childhood.

While growing up, the most influential people in my life were my mother, Jackie, my father, JB Sr., and my brother, Austin. I am not sure if I have ever formally vocalized it, but I learned something from each of them. During my youth, I was extremely inquisitive—some things do not change. My inquisitive nature led to me watching each of them very closely. I learned compassion from my mother, drive from my father, and hard work and mental toughness from my brother. One thing about my brother, he showed me tough love.

On most occasions during my brother's "tough love sessions," two things were certain to occur—I would shed tears, and he would tell me to quit b******* and man up! Many of these lessons took place on the basketball court. Oddly enough, he never played the sport.

Nevertheless, we would play a game of one-on-one,[18] and he would intentionally knock me down. At this time in my life, my brother was much larger than I, and he prided himself on his physical physique, which was probably the football player in him. Needless to say, when he knocked me down, it hurt. He would stand over me and tell me to get back up and finish the game. I did not realize until later on in life that he was not really teaching me how to be a better basketball player. Instead, he was teaching me about life, particularly mental toughness.

This revelation came to me during one of my favorite pastimes, watching movies. Admittedly, I watch a lot of movies. One of my favorite characters is Rocky Balboa. In one particular scene in Rocky VI, Rocky is standing near an entrance of an alley talking to his son. In that scene he told his son that the world was an ugly place. It does not matter how big and brave you are, life will knock you down. He explained that life will keep you there if you are not resilient. Rocky ended the conversation with his son after attempting to explain the importance of being able to bounce back after negative things happened.

Rocky was alluding to mental toughness, and so was my brother Austin. In the movies, Rocky was not known for his astuteness, acumen or intellect, but here he said all the right things. Mental toughness allows us to withstand the cruelties and harsh realities of life. I learned

---

[18] A game of basketball in which only two individuals compete. The game continues until a predetermine score is reached.

how cruel the world could be and how vital mental toughness is at an early age.

When I was thirteen years old, I attended a middle school in Shelby County, Tennessee known for its basketball prowess. I was good enough to make the team, but in the coach's eyes, I was not ready to play any meaningful minutes. Who am I kidding? I did not get in the game at all. There was a running joke about my lack of playing time — who would get in the game first, Smiley or the water boy? I would laugh it off, but the truth of the matter is that it bothered me more than I would admit at the time. Despite the comments, I would not be deterred from doing what I loved to do — playing basketball. Although I did not get in the game, I would practice as hard and more than anyone else. On game day, I would cheer from the bench as loud as I could for one of my closest friends, who happened to be the star player on the team.

My friend did not take basketball as serious as I did. I'm not sure if anyone did because we were only middle school kids, but he was admittedly better. He was about 6'0, athletic, and could physically dominate about ninety percent of 9th graders, and we were only in the 8th grade.

As the season began, we (by we I mean my teammates) dominated the competition. My friend was particularly impressive on defense and offense. The days following games were always exciting for those who played. The teachers and students would compliment them on how well they played. The compliments seemed to go in my friend's ear and out of the other. He did not care about the popularity or the attention he was receiving from the girls in our school. Honestly, I am not sure if he paid much attention to the high school coaches that were coming to our games to watch him play. He was nonchalant about those things. That is just who he was. I wished my coach would have known.

One day, the coach called my friend into the office. He fussed at him about something that had occurred during the school day. My friend did not take it well. He stormed out of the coach's office and indicated he was quitting the team. After practice, my coach called me into his office. I was not sure what he wanted or what he had to say, but for some reason I was nervous. What he said next proved I had every reason to be.

He said, "Smiley go get your boy, and bring him back." I then asked him what if he does not come back. He told me, "You might as well join him." My coach explained further that there was no room for me on the team unless I convinced my friend to rejoin. This was a difficult pill for me to swallow. My heart was racing, and my mind was full of thoughts—*should I tell my parents how the coach was manipulating me? Should I quit the team because it was obvious that the coach did not care whether I was a part of it or not? Or, should I convince my friend to do something he did not want to do so that I could continue to doing what I love?* Ultimately, I decided to convince my friend to rejoin the team. I never told a soul about the meeting with my coach until a few years ago. I was able to endure this type of manipulation and stress at an early age because of the preliminary lessons from my brother about being mentally tough and always getting back up. I am not sure what would have come of the situation if I was not mentally prepared for this thing we call life.

Mental Toughness and Its Stages of Development

I have some good news and some bad news. The good news, mental toughness is a facet of our inherent power. We do not have to go to Walmart or any other store that provides most of life's essentials to obtain it because we already have it. In fact, we were born with it. The bad news, well it is not really bad, but simply the truth. This power we possess, mental toughness, will need developing.

Developing mental toughness is vital. Our long-term and short-term success is contingent upon it. To properly develop it, you must first be mindful of the significance of mental toughness. You will need it when you fail your first test. You will need it when you lose a loved one. You will need it when you are wrongfully denied a promotion. You will need it when you are ridiculed because of your size. You will need it when you are discriminated against because you look a certain way or affiliated with a certain group. You will need it when you are surrounded by negativity looking for a way out. You will need it in all aspects of your life.

One of the key distinctions between those who excel and exceed expectations and those who settle or consistently come up short is mental toughness – the ability to bounce back when life happens. We cannot afford to take for granted, and we must develop this aspect of our psyche. Our success depends on it! Development of this power is not instantaneous. It will take time and will happen in stages. The first of which is, "my life is over." The second stage is "apprehensive." The final stage is "ready for the world." It cannot be denied that we all go through the first two stages at some point in our lives. But not all of us get to the final stage, ready for the world. The key to continued improvement is consistent development. Before consistent development is expounded upon, we must address the first two stages.

My life is over. There is no shame in admitting it; we have all said it or at least had the thought. This belief, my life is over, usually comes when our life is about to shift course. If you are reading this and can honestly say that you have not been here, keep living because I can almost promise you it is coming. The best thing for you to do is get prepared and keep reading, so it does not hit you like it hit me.

While growing up, one of my goals was to play professional basketball. So as you can imagine, I had a basketball in my hand at an early age, four to be exact. From the age of four on up, I played every year. Not only did I play during the school year, but I also played during the summers for several different AAU teams. The tryouts were full of the best players from the city and surrounding areas. It goes without saying, my AAU teams were full of talent, from the best point guard I ever played with Maurice "Moe" Miller to the best forward I ever played with Thaddeus "Thad" Young.

Before high school, I was good enough to make the team but never truly the star player. My brother told me if I wanted to make the high school team, I had to be the hardest working player in the city. He told me he was only 5'9, and there was no guarantee I would get any taller. As such, I began dribbling a mile a day, rain, sleet, or snow. I would spend countless hours in the front yard improving my jump shot. I can recall times in which my friends were heading to the Majestic movie theater in East Memphis to meet some girls, but I would decline and head to a nearby gymnasium to challenge some of the best basketball players in the city. I was committed to becoming a better basketball player. Basketball was my passion. Basketball was my first love.

Although I ended up growing to be a few inches taller than my brother, the preparation I put into becoming a better basketball player paid off. I was the only freshman to play Junior Varsity at Bolton High School, which was the largest high school in Shelby County at the time. Between my freshman and junior year, I witnessed some of the people I grew up competing with and against on the basketball court lose interest in the game. But not me, my love for the game only blossomed. I practiced harder and longer during that time. I reaped the benefits of my labor; my performance on the court improved as each year passed. By the end of my junior year, the newspapers in the city and surrounding areas started to take notice. At the conclusion of my senior year, I was selected as a member of the All-Shelby Metro team by the Commercial Appeal. According to the experts who selected the team, I was one of the best players in the area. This was a big deal, especially growing up in a city where basketball was the most popular sport.

As expected, my career continued in college. The first three years, I attended Tennessee Technological University, which is a mid-major NCAA Division 1 school in Cookeville, TN. Things did not go as expected during my time there, but my love for the game, although tested, remained. At the end of my junior year, I transferred to the University of Pikeville, which is a NAIA Division 1 school in Eastern Kentucky. During the summer while visiting my family and friends back home, I suffered an injury to my ankle. The podiatrist suggested I sit out an entire year so that I could fully recover. But of course, I did not want to take a year off from the game. I asked him was it possible for me to return any sooner. He explained that I could return to the court sooner if I were open to getting a cortisone injection and did not mind playing in some pain. Anyone that knows me knows how much I despise needles, but you know what they say, love conquers all. I may or may not have screamed, "Oh Lord," as the doctor was prepping to deliver the injection. It is quite possible I was so loud that the nurse came looking for a woman and found me instead.

After sitting out slightly over six weeks, I returned to the basketball court. I was in more pain than I expected, but I was happy to be back on the court nonetheless. I limped up and down the court with a smile on my face. One of my teammates, who eventually became one of my closest friends, gave me the nickname "peg leg." It did not matter to me if I was peg leg or peg legs as long as I was on the basketball court doing what I love. I eventually became numb to the pain and my performance on the court reflected that. I was able to help lead my team to twenty plus victories.

Upon college graduation, I played professional show basketball for the Harlem Ambassadors for several months. Then, I went to Mexico to play in a few exhibition games. When I decided that Mexico was not for me, I came back home. Eventually, I received another opportunity to play. This time, it was semi-professional basketball in the ABA. I left Memphis and moved to Avon Park, Florida for the opportunity. To make a long story short, I had the best season of my career. I averaged 23.2 points per game, five rebounds, and six assists. During the final game of that season, I scored a career high 46 points along with seven assists. When I left the ABA, I had no doubt my basketball career would continue, and I would end up in Europe.

I left Avon Park at the end of May and moved back to Memphis to train. I trained twice a day. During the morning training sessions, I ran hills, lifted weights, and played pick-up.[19] The evening training sessions consisted of skill work. I was in tip-top shape, and I have never been better on the basketball court. I was ready. In the beginning, I rarely contacted my agent because I knew the big deal was coming.

The closer it got to October, the more anxious I had become. As such, the frequency of my communication with my agent picked up. I called or emailed him

---

[19] Pick-up is a recreational game of basketball.

practically every day. By the time October had passed, most of my colleagues had signed contracts and were playing professionally in Europe. However, I was still at home without a deal. My parents, colleagues, and loved ones told me not to worry, and I would surely get a contract after the season I just had. I continued to train, and I prayed every night that my dreams of playing in Europe would come true.

The contract never came. My prayers were never answered. I was devastated. I am not sure if I have ever been depressed, but if I had been, it was at that time. I moped around and lied in the bed for the most of the day. I was too embarrassed to go anywhere because I did not want to be asked any basketball related questions. Mentally, I was defeated. I had given up. I had been playing basketball all my life. It was all I knew. It was my identity. I vividly remember lying in bed late one night, and my only thought was, "My life is over."

When I think about that moment in my life, I often wonder how I got there. My career had to end at some point. Why was I not prepared? The truth is, it did not matter when it ended because the development of my mental toughness ended with those lessons with my brother. Okay, enough sugar coating, I was mentally weak. If you ever said, "My life is over" or if the thought ever crossed your mind, you were too.

Apprehensive. This stage of mental toughness is also called the "I'm not so sure stage." Think about it. What's stopping or hindering you from taking advantage of all this world has to offer? Is it your co-workers? How about your boss? Maybe it is your friends? It is none of those individuals; it's you! When you are at this stage you allow fear of rejection, failure, or disappointment keep you complacent, stagnant, or from taking any risks despite the potential for financial gain, mental or physical satisfaction, or success. You are unsure of yourself.

You know when you are at this stage. Your reasons for doing, more frequently not doing, tell the story. It is a story familiar to us all. You are presented with an opportunity that could be potentially beneficial; the same opportunity could be a dead end. Instead of thoroughly thinking through the advantages and disadvantages, or assuming the best, you dwell on the potential for failure. At this point, you decide not to take action, and you come up with a justification that leaves you at peace with your decision. Then, if someone made the opportunity available, you give such excuse to the person. This cycle repeats invariably.

When you are at this stage, it is also evident to those who interact with you. What you say and what you do, paint the picture. They see someone who is indecisive. Because you are viewed as someone who is indecisive or lacks confidence, fewer opportunities to lead will come your way. As a result, the opportunities available to you will have glass ceilings or no upward mobility. Your attitude or lack of mental toughness has effectively subjected you to mediocrity.

In order to fight off or avoid being labeled apprehensive, it is quite possible you outwardly manifest a false sense of security. It is also likely that you indicate you are carefully considering as opposed to being apprehensive, although the latter is true. It should be noted that there is a difference between being apprehensive and carefully considering. You should spend time assessing or contemplating what you want and where you want to be. This greatly reduces the likelihood of backtracking, which is usually associated with arbitrary decisions. On the other hand, apprehension is anxiety or thought centered around a potential negative outcome. The key distinction between the two is, carefully considering necessitates a contemplation of the totality of the circumstances with the appropriate weight given to each possibility. There is absolutely nothing wrong with carefully considering before making a decision. In fact, it is encouraged. However, be careful not to confuse the two.

During this stage, many times, you say things or take positions contrary to how you actually feel because you want to be seen in a positive light. You want others to see you as a confident individual. Hence, you begin to say things like, "Let me consider it" or "Let me sleep on it" rather than "I am not so sure." You say, " I can handle it" rather than "I am probably not the person for the job." This is dangerous, dishonest, and disadvantageous.

You are probably thinking, how is it dangerous? How is it dishonest? How could it possibly be disadvantageous? It is dangerous because you could jeopardize your livelihood. If you underperform or fail to perform at all due to your lack of confidence, you may not get another opportunity. It is dishonest because you are essentially lying to yourself and pretending to be someone you are not. It is disadvantageous because by putting forth this façade it is possible you begin to believe it and/or never fully address your current mental state. If you never fully address your current mental state or lack of mental toughness, you will forever be in this state of apprehensiveness.

One question remains: how do you fully address it, through consistent development.

Consistent Development does not just happen. Although, it would be much easier if it did. But that is not how it works. As indicative by the word consistent, growth in the area of mental toughness will require continuous development. Your mind has to be trained so that your will can be strong. A man far wiser than I once said, "Strength does not come from physical capacity. It comes from an indomitable will."[20]

One of my mentors was a firm believer in being proactive to prepare his student-athletes for what was ahead, adulthood. He often said, "Proper preparation prevents piss poor performance." At first, I did not think much of it other than he wanted us to be prepared on the basketball court. Eventually, my inquisitive nature got the best of me. During a conversation with him, I brought up his favorite saying. He told me that he was in the business of grooming student-athletes so that they would be prepared for the real world. As he continued to talk, I was uncertain what any of it had to do with his famous saying. Of course, I expressed my uncertainty to him. He chuckled a bit, and said that it should be applied to all areas of our

---

[20] This quote is attributed to Mahatma Gandhi.

lives, both physical and mental. What he was alluding to was that proper preparation for life included developing mentally so that we can endure the trials and tribulations that were sure to come.

Indeed, success on any level or with regard to any goal requires mental toughness. Athletes go through mental toughness development as part of the training process. For example, basketball players are expected to run sprints until they can barely stand. They are usually gasping for air and wanting water. At this point, the coach usually beacons to one of the players to shoot a freethrow. In order to make the freethrow, the player has to overcome any physical or mental fatigue to hit the shot. Additionally, the coach adds pressure by requiring the team to run more sprints if the player misses the shot. The ultimate goal is for the players to eventually make freethrows despite mental and physical fatigue and the added pressure. This process continues until the team hits a certain number of freethrows.

Analogous to the coach requiring his basketball players to make freethrows while under various pressures, both physical and mental, we too must set goals and practice overcoming the circumstances. There are several ways you can properly develop your mental toughness; below, you will find my approach.

Level 1

Begin developing your mental toughness by setting a goal unrelated to anything of significance in your life, which I refer to as level 1. However, there needs to be some form of physical or mental pressure associated with the goal. If you are a person, who spends most weekdays in an office setting rarely working out, begin your training by setting a goal that will require physical activity outside for three days a week for at least thirty minutes. If this is too difficult, you can begin with a less strenuous goal. This can be accomplished by reducing the number of days or time spent working out. The important thing is to set a small realistic goal and achieve it in spite of your daily stressors. Once you have accomplished this goal repeatedly without failing, you are ready to move on to your next test, Level 2.

Level 2

Level two requires you to set a goal that has both physical and mental pressures as opposed to one or the other. This goal should also be unrelated to anything significant in your life. The difficulty of completing the goal should be more strenuous than the previous one. For example, if you are a person who rarely reads, set a goal to read at least ten pages of a book every night. You will likely be physically and mentally tired by the end of your day and reading ten pages of a book will be the last thing you want to do. You have to train yourself to persevere, and this is just another stepping-stone in your preparation. Similar to level one, you have to accomplish this goal consistently before moving on to the final stage of preparation, level three.

Level 3

Level three is the last step in your mental preparation. Your level three-goal must have both physical and mental pressures. In addition to the mental and physical pressures, there must be something at stake. The goal must relate to something that has a direct impact on your life. The goal must be something you have control over. It cannot be something contingent on another person. Perhaps, you are trying to purchase your first car or house; you can set a goal to save a feasible amount of money each month.

I would be remiss if I did not remind you that life happens even after you set goals. A family member will call you needing money, your friends will want to take a vacation, your significant other will want a pricey gift, and you may want to do all those things. However, to accomplish your goal, you will have to make sacrifices. Not everyone will understand, and some may distance themselves, but that should be expected. Accomplishing your goal should take precedence. If it does not, and you fail to accomplish your goal due to external or internal influences, you are in danger of becoming passive when it comes to your personal goals. If you become passive in that regard, you are settling for less. This will begin a cycle of continued failures and mediocrity. You cannot allow this to happen.

Level three's purpose is to prepare you mentally to endure life's hard times, overcome life's obstacles, and generally get you mentally tough. Set feasible goals. Accomplish those goals. Once you have repeatedly done so, eventually accomplishing your goals will become a habit even in the midst of the strongest storm. At this point, you will be ready for the world.

Ready for the world. When you are truly ready for the world, it does not matter what comes your way, what setback you experience, or the severity of the storm you are going through because you refuse to be denied. Maya Angelou said it best, "We may encounter defeats, but we must not be defeated." You cannot effectively utilize your inherent power unless you reach this level of mental maturity. It took some time for me to get to that point. Ironically, my basketball career coming to an end was the catalyst.

I felt defeated. My dreams of continuing my basketball career seemed to be shattered. As I stated earlier, I thought to myself, "My life is over." But that was not the case. My life was getting ready to take a turn for the best.

I did not tell anyone how miserable I was. Actually, I was able to fake a smile for the most part. My friends would call, and eventually I became more social. Most of the social events I attended had loud music, but not loud enough to drown out my inner thoughts of worthlessness. I was walking around the city frequenting social events without a job or career, and I was no longer an athlete. I felt out of place. The truth is, I was not the only one in this predicament, and knowing that did nothing for me mentally. I was still in a state of despair. Although I felt this way, there was something in me saying, you may have suffered a loss, but you have not lost.

I wanted to do more, but I was apprehensive about refocusing. I attempted to run from my problems. I took trips, visited friends, and had a lot of fun trying to escape my current circumstances. After the trips, my money started to run low. Instead of truly refocusing, I began searching for jobs although I did not see a future at any of them. I was not only seeking a means of income, but I was also looking for a "hideout." A place I could go and hide from myself. I knew my family and friends would think that I was looking for a job and attempting to better myself. I knew they would be proud. Regardless of how my loved ones felt, the reason I was seeking a job was nothing to be proud of. The job would be my hideout. I was hiding because I was scared to refocus and set another goal. I thought setting another goal would only lead to failure.

Not long after I began my search, I found a hideout. I started training with the company shortly after that. At the end of the training, there was a written examination; I made a perfect score. The higher ups in the company seemed to be excited to have me aboard, but I was indifferent. The first couple of weeks went by extremely slow. I stared at the clock for long periods wishing it would go faster.

One morning, as I reluctantly prepared for work, I contemplated quitting. Suddenly, it dawned on me that I was settling and not living up to my own expectations. I asked myself if I wanted to continue running and hiding or if I was ready to refocus. Before I made a decision, I started reflecting back on the things I had to endure and how hard I had to work just to have an opportunity to play professional show basketball and semi-professional basketball. I realized I was not a failure at all but an overcomer. The decision was made; it was time to refocus. At that very moment, I knew I was more than capable of handling whatever life had in store for me — good or bad. I was ready for the world.

Although it took some time for me to get to the point where I was mentally prepared for whatever life had in store, I got there. I am confident you will too. If your current mental state is anything other than "ready for the world," do not be discouraged. Each and every person must go through some form of mental development in order to excel. He who fails to develop mentally fails to succeed. Stated more directly, if you lack mental toughness, your chances of succeeding are virtually nonexistent. Mental toughness is a necessary part of your personal success story. Once you have properly developed this part of your psyche, not only will you be ready for the world, you will be able to take control.

Chapter 4

Take Control

"Peak performance begins with you taking complete responsibility for your life and everything that happens to you."
– Brian Tracy

Freedom! Freedom! Freedom! You are probably wondering why I began a chapter titled "Take Control" by chanting Freedom! Well, here is why. Taking control of your life gives you freedom. By taking control, you create space to pursue the desires of your heart freely and decide the path you will take to reach your goals. When you "grab the bull by the horns," you gain the advantage and clarity needed to make tough choices regarding your education, career, finances, relationships, family, and your life. Taking control starts when you begin taking responsibility for your actions, decisions, mistakes, and most importantly, for the development of your future. If you are blaming someone else for your life situations or depending on someone else to make you successful, you are not taking control of your life.

All across America, there are teenagers in the 11th and 12th grade gearing up for their first real encounter with making major life-altering decisions. For some, they must decide which college or trade school to attend, while others consider joining the military or entering the workforce. Regardless of the path, students often struggle with taking control and commandeering life after high school. For me, the struggle was real.

After graduating high school, I could not wait to begin my college career. I am not sure if I was more excited about playing college basketball or becoming less dependent on my parents. I would be living on my own for the first time in my life. One thing was certain; I was ready to begin this chapter of my life, at least I thought so. I majored in Sociology[21] with a concentration in Criminal Justice.[22] I assumed that I would learn about human behavior as well as the ins and outs of the criminal justice system. However, I spent more time learning about myself and attempting to take control of my life.

This was necessary for me because most of my childhood, when it came time to make any decision of importance, my father had the final say. This trend continued when it was time to decide my next step after high school. I was seventeen and needed my parents to sign off on any decision, at least I thought I did. During the course of my senior season, I received strong interest from two NCAA Division I schools. One of the schools wanted me to attend prep school, which would allow me to

[21]   Sociology is defined as the science of society, social institutions, and social relationships; *specifically*: the systematic study of the development, structure, interaction, and collective behavior of organized groups of human beings.

[22]   When I transferred from Tennessee Technological University (TTU) after my junior year to the University of Pikeville, I changed my major from Sociology with a concentration in Criminal Justice to a doubled major, Sociology and Criminal Justice. I took over 20 hours of classes each semester. That year is a book in itself but I'll save it for my next book.

continue to develop physically. Notably, I graduated at the age of 17 and had not physically matured yet. The school went so far as to pick out the prep school in addition to telling me that my former high school rival and colleague would be joining me. I was eager about the potential to continue developing physically in prep school while honing my skills. I also looked forward to playing alongside my former rival, but then, my father happened.

He communicated with the coach and told him that prep school was for students who struggled in the classroom, and his son did not fall into that category. At the end of the conversation, my father told the coach that I would not be attending prep school or their university. My father only had my best interest at heart, but his knowledge of the game of basketball and the benefits of prep school were limited. In his mind, education was the only thing that mattered. In my mind, education and basketball both mattered, but he did not see it that way. When the other school began calling, my father simply told the coach they were too far away, and I needed to be much closer to the family.[23]

After turning down the two NCAA Division I schools that were genuinely interested in my talents, my father gathered all the information on my basketball career and sent it to Tennessee Technological University (TTU). I

[23] During the recruitment period, I made a few mistakes of my own. Whenever I would receive a letter from a Non-NCAA Division I School, I would simply discard it. If you reading this, and have aspirations to play college basketball, do not make the same mistake I made, and consider all options; after all, you are getting a free education.

attended TTU not because it was where I wanted to be but because my father wanted me there.

Limited Life

The word "take" precedes the word "control" in the title of this chapter, and it is not a coincidence or chance happening. It is intentional. It is there for a purpose. Before you can control anything, action is required. Hence, the action verb "take" preceding "control." You have to be proactive to take control of your life. It is not just going to happen. Being passive or nonchalant in this regard will lead to you living a "limited life."

But what is a "limited life?" A limited life consists of several shortcomings. It is a life full of excuses. It is a life full of regrets. It is a life always lived in the comfort zone. It is the life you live when you refuse to take responsibility for your actions or lack thereof. It is the life you live if you are allowing someone to take care of you when you are capable of doing so yourself. It is the life you live when you refuse to work. It is the life you live if you fail to discover your inherent power. It is the life you live when you do not strive for independence but content with dependence. It is the life you live when you refuse to step up to the plate and be a present mother or father. A limited life is not the life for you nor is it the life you were meant to live!

While I was in college, it dawned on me that I was living a limited life. But when I started college that was the furthest thing from my mind. I started college thinking I would learn about criminal justice and sociology while becoming a better basketball player. Although I did all of the above, the most important thing I did or learned could not be found in a textbook or on the basketball court. This was not a lesson my professor could teach nor could my coach instruct me in this regard. I had to learn this on my own. I had to learn it the old fashion way, experience, which led to self-reflection.

My journey to discovering that I was living a limited life, also known as the realization of how "trifling" I was, began my freshman year. On the outside, it appeared I was living my dream, but that could not be any further from the truth. During my freshman year, I went to class, made good grades, and attempted to prove myself on the basketball court. Basically, I did everything my parents expected of me. When they called, visited, or when I had the opportunity to go home I pretended all was well. I did not do this for my mom so to speak; I did this for my father. I knew he expected me to do all these things and not deviate from the path he wanted me to travel. To him and some of my siblings, I was the golden child. My brother, Austin, often teased and said if I made a mistake or did not live my life a certain way, I would not just be letting my mother and father down but my entire family. So, I continued to do what was expected. I lived my life constrained. I did not feel free to make any of my own decisions. I let my family dictate those.

I stayed the course all of my freshman year. During the summer, instead of recognizing or admitting that I was living a limited life, I continued to live life with my eyes closed. What I mean by that is, although I was living, I refused to see what was directly in front of me. I became obsessed with becoming stronger and faster while ignoring the other area of my life that needed attention. I went from 170 lbs soaking wet to around 185lbs prior to the start of my sophomore year.

My sophomore year was much of the same; well, at least it was at the outset. I went to class, made good grades, and attempted to prove myself on the basketball court. I even saw an increase in playing time. I did not deviate from the path expected, so I knew my family would be proud. But, I was still not happy.

Sometime during my sophomore year, I began hanging with my teammates, Derrick and Chris, on a regular basis. We all had different backgrounds. Chris was from St. Louis, Missouri and all over Arkansas. He had a difficult childhood, but that made him resilient. Derrick was from Warner Robbins, Georgia. He grew up with a very loving mother who was willing to do anything to see her children do well. He also experienced the worst type of loss; someone very close to him was murdered. This made Derrick appreciate life and want to live it the way he wanted and without any boundaries. Chris and Derrick stood 6'6 and 6'9 respectively. In hindsight, I did not know what I was getting myself into, but the lessons I learned from each of them prepared me for what I needed to do — take control.

Derrick had a very commanding presence. When people met him, male or female, they automatically respected him. Most of the time he did not have to say a word. What I thought to be peculiar was, it had less to do with the fact that he was 6'9 and more to do with the way he lived his life. He was the captain of his own ship, and I was not. Needless to say, I should have been taking notes. There were many occasions where Derrick would travel to Georgia, Chattanooga, or Nashville, just because he could. He would always ask me to come along. At first, I was hesitant to take trips without checking in; I played it cool though. You would have never known that I was checking in constantly, but the more I hung out with him, the more confident and comfortable I became choosing what is right for me.

I learned something different from Chris. Chris, like Derrick, was his own captain. Our coaches made jokes about Chris and would say, "It doesn't matter what we say, Chris is going to do what he wants to do." Although statements like that were made in jest, I am not sure if any statement could capture how Chris lived his life better than that. Chris was going to do what Chris was going to do. If he made a mistake, he lived with it and bounced back better than before. On one particular occasion during a scrimmage game against the University of Arkansas at Little Rock, I recall dribbling the ball up the court and passing the ball to Chris about 5 feet outside of the three point line. I am not sure how the play ended, but I recall my coach interrupting the scrimmage and yelling, "Chris, you will never, ever, ever, ever, play the three!"[24] Coach

---

[24] The "three" is basketball lingo for the small forward position. Small forwards are capable of dribbling the ball up the

immediately took both Chris and I out of the game. I hung my head, but Chris, although he was angry about being taken out of the game and being called out in front of everyone, said very confidently, "When I get back in I am going to prove that I can play the three." I learned from Chris that you do not have to be perfect. It is all right to make a mistake, but learn from it and improve the next time around.

I learned something extremely important from both Derrick and Chris. The lessons I learned from each of them helped me come to a very important conclusion; I relied on my family to dictate my course. In fact, I did more than acquiesce; I sought them out for direction and approval. I was reluctant to do anything outside of the box because I was afraid to make mistakes. Frankly, I was scared to be my own man. I was finally ready to admit, what I knew deep down inside, I was living a limited life. But seeing them walk unafraid of missteps and truly enjoying life and living free was all the push I needed. I was ready to take control.

Timeout! Yes, I am calling a timeout in the middle of a story, but for good reason. Taking control requires more than just making decisions of your own volition. If you choose to act without the proper amount of reflection, you can end up losing the thing you wanted most, control. One bad move without reflection is all that is needed for you to end up in jail, which is the most significant deprivation of control you can experience. The State or the

---

court if necessary. They are usually the most versatile player on the court.

United States will control your actions and interactions for a length of time, which will be contingent upon the severity of your mistake. The consequences of attempting to take control or making decisions without adequate reflection do not necessarily have to be that harsh. Sometimes the consequences just hurt your pocket. Like most of the things I learned in undergrad, I had to learn this lesson the hard way.

After I began to experience what control felt like, I started making more and more decisions without relying on my family nearly as much as I did in the past. My problem with taking control began for two reasons: I enjoyed making decisions for myself too much, and while I was making those decisions, I did not give them much thought. I was in for a rude awakening.

In 2007, something big happened. Well, it was big to those of us loyal to T-mobile. T-mobile unveiled its newest Sidekick cell phone, the Sidekick Lx. It was a must have. I did not have much money, but the money I did have I spent it on that phone and did not consult anyone about it. One of my younger teammates also wanted the Sidekick Lx. He bought the phone but could not get a line because his credit was non-existent. I am not sure if I had sucker written on my forehead or what, but he asked me if I would allow him to get a phone line on my account. He told me he would pay the bill on time and would never be late. I told him to let me think about it (I should have thought longer). Shortly after I left T-mobile, I received a call from my mother. I think she could sense I was about to make a poor decision. While we were on the phone, I told her I was considering getting an additional line for my teammate. Before I could even finish telling her all of the background information, she interrupted me and said, "Do not do it. You will regret it." When I asked her why, she said, "If he does not pay, you will be stuck with not only the phone bill but also with the disconnection fee." I should have listened!

Thinking I was ready to take control of my life, I allowed my younger teammate to join my account and get an additional line. I made that decision just because my mother advised against it (this is never a good reason to do anything). I thought I would show her she did not always know best. The first couple of months went like clockwork. Then he started making payments that were a week or so behind. When I noticed the delayed payments, I approached him, and he assured me that he would always pay. I am not sure if I believed him or if I just wanted to believe him because I did not want my mother to be right. Either way, the account stayed open. It was time for the next payment, and he asked if I would pay it for him this time, and the next time he would pay both my bill and his. I agreed. Surprisingly, the next time around he kept his word and paid both bills. This trend continued for the two months. I would pay his bill, and then he would pay mine. Then it happened; he completely missed a payment. He continued to assure me he would have the money to pay, but he did not. He told me he would pay the remaining balance and the disconnection fee. He did not.

After a few weeks had gone by, I called T-mobile to get the remaining balance on his line, and I also inquired about the disconnection fee. The T-mobile associate told me the total bill for disconnecting that line in addition to the remaining balance on the account was in excess of $500.00. I literally almost screamed. I was a broke college kid and did not have that type of money lying around. But not wanting to tell my mother what happened, I went to my younger teammate and asked when he would have the money. He told me soon. To this day, I have never seen the money or heard anything else about it. It was time for me to bite the bullet and confess to my mother.

Before I called my mother, I began prepping for our conversation. During my prepping session, I thought about deceiving her and telling her I needed the money for some other purpose. After all, I was her baby boy; she would believe me right? Here lies the dilemma: I was pretty sure my mother was the human lie detector, and even if her uncanny ability to figure out when I am not completely forthcoming failed, she would be worried that I had bad habits that needed to be addressed. I decided to come clean. I picked up the phone and called her. She answered the phone in such a pleasant manner. Too bad I was getting ready to ruin it.

I tried to finesse my way around the real reason for the call. I asked and discussed every topic I could think of before telling my mother about my foolish act. I asked about how things were going, and what was the last movie she saw. I am pretty sure the fact that my mother never goes to the movies tipped her off that I was calling for some other purpose yet stated. In her typical fashion when she knows I am beating around the bush so to speak, she interrupted me mid-sentence and said, "Boy what do you want?" I immediately got quiet. The longer I stayed silent, the more outlandish my mother's guesses became as she tried to figure out the reason for the call. Finally, I told her. Like any other person who is getting ready to make the biggest excuse of his or her life, my explanation began with, "See what had happened was..."

I did not tell my mother how hardheaded I was, how I was rebelling, or how I made a decision without proper reflection. She already knew. By the time I finished telling my mother about my predicament, I had accepted the fact that a lecture from my mother was soon to follow. As she had done some many times before, she agreed to help but not before she lectured me. Her lecture was not filled with, "I told you so's" nor did it contain any put downs, she as only a mother could do, explained to me in a loving way that my downfall was the lack of proper reflection.

Proper Reflection

During grade school, most of us were taught a simple concept, "Think before you speak," which was explained over a few days. What should have been included in the lessons or given a lesson of its own is a similar idea called, "Think before you Act." As elementary as it may seem, this concept is equally important and should be applied to matters of adult concern. Although it took a lecture from my mother about its importance, which was probably longer and more thorough than any lesson I would receive in school due to the time constraints and the number of students being taught, I admittedly should have known better.

We are all born with one of the most influential forces known to man, a conscience. It's the voice inside of us saying, "You better not do that!" or "Are you sure you want to do this?" It's this inner voice that tells you to think before you act or as coined in this book, proper reflection.

As explained to me by my mother with a few added things I have picked up along my journey, the first thing you must do when you are properly reflecting is ask yourself why do you want to act. If the answer does not consist of a proper motive, you should not be acting. Please note, if the sole reason you want to act is to prove someone wrong, my friend, you do not have a proper motive. I am sure some of you may still be having trouble deciding if your motive is a proper one. Hence, I have included a list of proper motives: bettering yourself, which includes studying, becoming physically fit, eating healthy, seeking independence, improving your critical thinking skills, becoming financially stable, enhancing your career, pursuing your passion or seeking spiritual growth, or desiring to help someone. If the motive behind your act does not fall in either of the above categories, your motive is likely a frivolous one.

The next thing you should do is weigh the pros and cons. This is when you compare and contrast the advantages and disadvantages of your proposed action. While doing this, you also take into consideration whether you can live with the potential consequences of such action. Although I believe it could go without saying, I find it necessary to mention the following in spite of that. All actions, good or bad, or with a proper or frivolous motive, have consequences. Therefore, consequences must be accounted for.

The final thing you should do when properly reflecting is choose action or inaction. At this point, you should be more than prepared to make a decision based on sound reasoning. Whatever you decide, action or inaction, do it confidently knowing that you have properly reflected, prepared to reap any reward, and are ready to live with any consequences that may come your way. Proper reflection is one of the few things in this life that transcends age, color, sexual orientation, or religion. We all need it and are born with a conscience telling us to reflect properly.

After making several ill-advised decisions thinking I was ready to take control, I took a step back and listened. It was at this point that I started listening to my conscience and began properly reflecting before making any momentous decisions. I was truly ready to take control now. The first significant decision I made while applying the steps listed above occurred my junior year of college.

My junior year was different from any year I had prior. I entered my junior year fully expecting to play a vital on-court role in our team's success, but this was not the case. My time on the floor actually decreased from the previous season. For the first time in my life, I was unhappy both on and off the basketball court. Basketball was no longer my sanctuary. I began to dread going to practice. My teammates could even see the difference in the way that I played the game. Normally, I played the game with so much passion; my competitive spirit would rub off on my teammates. I would guard the ball handler the entire length of the court. My teammates and coaches expected me to be that player. However, I was no longer that player. I felt like I was falling out of love with my first love, the game of basketball, but I knew that was not the case.

I knew I had to do something. I had to take control. I began thinking about ways to remedy the situation. The answer became clear. I needed to transfer. I discussed the decision with two of my closest teammates at the time, Derrick and Chris of course. Although Derrick, our star player, did his best Johnnie Cochran imitation when attempting to convince me why staying would be a better decision, he said he understood. When discussing a potential transfer with Chris, he stated that he was actually considering the same.

After discussing a potential transfer with Derrick and Chris, I began weighing the pros and cons. The answer seemed clear; transferring was the thing to do. There were still three important things left to do: tell my parents, tell my coaches, and find the right school for myself. As it relates to my coaches and how you should conduct yourself, I did not go about transferring in the most professional manner. Let's just say it was a mutual decision (If you want to find out what went down, you will have to buy my next book assuming I write another or just ask me in person). I still had to tell my parents. Of course, I decided to push that off a little longer until I had a few potential schools in mind.

It did not take long for me to gather a list of schools willing to pay for my education if I agreed to attend and play basketball for their institution. After I had narrowed my list to three schools, I decided to do what my brother calls, "Manning up!" I called my parents to inform, not ask, about my decision to transfer.

I called my mother first. When I told her about my decision, the first thing she said was "Did you tell your daddy." I am uncertain what was said next, but some way or another I ended up on the phone with my father. He asked me if I had lost my mind. He was adamant I "stay put." His firm belief that I was currently attending the best school for me remained unwavering, so did my conviction about transferring. Needless to say, the conversation ended on a sour note.

Despite the fact that my father did everything but forbid my transfer, I continued in that direction. Not long after getting my release, I decided to visit a few of the schools on my list. Something that surprised but encouraged me to stay the course was that one of the coaches came to me in confidence and told me that I was making the best decision for me. He even offered to help me find another school to continue my career. I thanked him for the offer, but I informed him I needed to make this decision on my own.

After choosing my top two schools, I called my father once more. I informed him that I would be visiting the schools at the top of my list. I told him I planned to visit those schools on specified dates. He asked to come, as I knew he would. He could not turn down the opportunity to show me why I should stay put. What he did not know was, I could not turn down the chance to show him that transferring was the best decision for me.

Jurisdiction

Jurisdiction is one of the most frequently used words in the legal profession. When lawyers or legal scholars use the word jurisdiction, he or she is usually referring to the court's power to exercise authority over someone or something. In every lawsuit filed, the first document sent to the court should address why the court has jurisdiction. You are probably thinking I worked jurisdiction into this book because I'm a lawyer; that is only partially true. In all seriousness, jurisdiction does have value in this context as well.

In this context, jurisdiction represents your power to exercise authority over your life and the things that affect it. Once you have rid yourself of the mental shackles that make up a limited life and begin to properly reflect before acting, you transition from existing to living. You are ready to exercise jurisdiction not only over your life but also over those things that affect it.

For me, my transition occurred when visiting the two schools at the top of my transfer list with my father. Before this trip with my father, I thought I was ready to take control. I figured that I freed myself from the "limited life" in which I allowed others to make meaningful decisions for me. There was one impediment that stood between me and what I sought, which was true control over my life, and it had nothing to do with my father.

I was eager for the visits to begin. Up first was the second school on my list. Once we arrived on campus, the head coach greeted us. I was all smiles. My father, on the other hand, was all business. I do not believe he smiled or smirked the entire trip. Shortly after being greeted by the head coach, the team's star player showed us around the living area where I would be staying if I chose to sign with the school. Every time, I saw something nice or beneficial, I would look at my father seeking approval. I could not read him. Either he was unimpressed, or he had the best poker face ever during this trip. If I were an optimist as opposed to a realist, I would go with the latter. I knew my father was not going to change his opinion that easy.

Sometime before the end of the visit, my father and I went into the coach's office. Although I was diligently listening, (if you do not remember what this is, See Chapter 1) every time the coach would say something appealing, I could not help but glance over at my father. I was hoping he would smile, smirk, or give me some indication that I was making the right decision. Nope! He still was unimpressed. I went so far as to ask the coach what he could do for me. I did not ask the question necessarily to get good responses; I asked it more so for my benefit. I thought my father would be proud I was bold enough to ask that question. To my surprise, the coach responded that he would be able to get me a brand new laptop if I decided to transfer to the school. I decided to push my luck; I asked if he could arrange it so I could work in a law firm while I was in school there. The coach said if I could give him a week, he could work something out. At the conclusion of visit one, my father did not have much to say.

It was time to visit the second school, which was first on my list. This time one of my older brothers also accompanied us. Similar to the first school, the head coach also greeted us. He showed us around the campus. However, knowing that academia was also important to my family and I, he took us to meet the president of the University. The president was brilliant. He dazzled us with conversations that ranged from past Rhodes scholars to the current state of basketball. He assured me that my time at their institution would consist of fine learning and a great experience on the basketball court. After leaving the president's office, I believed that signing there would be the right decision. Nevertheless, I was still seeking approval from my brother and father.

For the rest of the visit, I continued to think about how I could convince my father and brother that this was the right decision. Sometime during the visit, I was informed that I could work in a law firm and receive college credit. This was a dream come true. Although I was ready to sign at that point, I felt like I still needed approval from my family. At the conclusion of the visit, I asked my father what he thought about the schools. He told me he still believed TTU was the place for me, but the other schools were alright. But this was not good enough for me. I was seeking his validation.

After we had gone our separate ways, my father and brother back to Memphis, and I back to Cookeville, TN, I sat in my apartment for a day or so contemplating what went wrong. I asked myself why was I not able to convince him that either school was a better option for me at this point. I placed both scholarship packets on my desk and left them there until the start of the next week. I thought taking some time away from the stressors associated with this decision would do me some good.

When the next week began, I was still reluctant to sign in spite of the opportunities the other schools were offering. The school on the top of my list would actually give me an opportunity to be more than just an athlete. It would truly allow me to become a student-athlete. I could add an additional major and still graduate on time. I could work in a law firm and determine if it was the profession I wanted to take up after my basketball career comes to an end (For all of my athletes reading this, there is always an "after" when dealing with sports. Plan and prepare for it). Last but certainly not least, I would have an opportunity to play meaningful minutes on the hardwood, and compete for a winning program.

As soon as I finished thinking about the opportunities before me, I made a concerted effort to figure out what was hindering my decision. I knew the hindrance was mental but was not quite sure how to address it nor was I certain what it was. For some reason or another, I began reflecting back on how I acted during the visit. I realized that every time I was impressed by something said or done on the visits, I would look to my father for validation. I would look to him as if I was a boy, not a man. I was looking at him the same way a child around elementary school age would look at his or her parent when it was time for them to eat. You see, the elementary age child is not capable of providing for him or herself; they need their parents to make these decisions for them. But I was certainly not an elementary age child. I was fully capable of making my own decisions, and there was no reason for me to seek validation.

Without further delay, I picked up the pen, signed the document reflecting the scholarship to the school on the top of my list, and promptly mailed it. This was the happiest moment of my life, not because of the scholarship to the school of my choice, but because I was exercising jurisdiction over those things that affected me. I was finally in control. The next day, I called my parents and informed them of my decision. When they both could hear me, I boldly said, "I will be attending Pikeville College."[25] I am not sure which one of my parents made the next comment, but the next thing I heard was, "Are you asking or telling?" I responded, "Neither, just informing." I chuckled. My father said, "I see you have made your decision, so there is nothing left for me to say other than I wish you luck son." I told my father, "I do not need luck because I am ready for whatever this world has in store for me, good or bad." Of course, I did not make that statement to my father, but the thought sure did come into my head. What I did say was thanks for being there all these years. I

---

[25] Pikeville College later changed it name to the University of Pikeville.

believe my mother knew that was my way of telling my father I do not need him to serve as my final decision maker any longer, and I was ready to step up to the plate. My mother knew I was ready to take control. I was not sure if my father would ever have this epiphany, but that's okay, I knew I was still ready.

Taking control of your life and exercising jurisdiction over the things that affect it are essential to your transition from merely existing to truly living. When you make the transition from living a limited life to a life full of purpose and freedom, you will begin to approach life differently than you did before. Your new approach to life will yield positive results, and you alone will be responsible. New opportunities will present themselves and doors once closed will open. You will not have to demand or ask for respect. The way in which you carry yourself will be a catalyst for the respect you receive in your personal life and professionally as well.

You will know when you have seized control of your life because you will echo these sentiments: I'd rather fail attempting to live my dream than be successful living someone else's!

Section 3: Maximizing Your Inherent Power

"One step toward a goal is better than any moment of complacency." Just a couple of years ago while talking with a friend on the phone, attempting to encourage him, I said those very words. At that time, I did not realize the significance of the statement. It embodies the mindset of every ambitious business owner, entrepreneur, young professional, college student, service-member, and goal-oriented person. It is essentially what every person attempting to take the next step in his or her chosen path should be thinking. However, if you are not there yet, do not be discouraged. It took me a while to get there as well.

It was the summer of 2011, I was twenty-three, had been out of college for two plus years, and I was still living at home. During that summer, a friend of mine from out of town came to visit. When he arrived, I was excited to show him what Memphis had to offer. Like most Memphians my age, I took him to historic Beale Street. While there, two extremely beautiful ladies caught our eyes. Approaching them was no problem. I actually knew one of the ladies from high school. Our conversation with the ladies revealed that they had careers and did not live with their parents. Also apparent was my friend's interest in one of the ladies. Like a good host and in an attempt to impress my friend, I invited the ladies over. They accepted the invitation. We rushed to my house to prepare for their arrival. Shortly after we finished cleaning, the doorbell rang; they had arrived. As I opened the door, they stepped in. The girl who entered first quickly looked around and said, "Whose momma's house is this?" My friend quickly said he was from out of town, and it was not his mother's house. What my friend left out of his explanation was that he currently lived with his parents as well. But it was at that moment I had an epiphany, getting out of my mother's house was a priority and being complacent was not the solution. My goals and priorities became apparent. I had to get from Point A to Point B.

No matter where you are in your career or personal life, you must face and answer the quintessential question, not "Whose momma's house is this," but the same question I asked myself after hearing the young lady's remark — "How do I get from Point A to Point B?" Success is a direct and derivative result of your answer to this very specific question. Let me explain. Point A is where you are now. Point B, for some, might consist of starting your own business and for others, it may be getting out of your mother's house. Hence, Point B is the next step.

In order to get to Point B, you must keep in mind and commit to heart three basic principles: (1) know what you want, (2) focus on what you want, and (3) be determined to achieve it. "Knowing what you want" means identifying your end goal. "Focusing on what you want" means making your end goal a priority. "Being determined to achieve it" means being intentional in all that you do with the aim of bringing about the end result — achieving your goal.

Chapter 5

Know What You Want

"The future belongs to those who prepare for it today." –
Malcolm X

In the introduction to this section, I stated that knowing what you want is identifying your end goal. However, I did not explain what an end goal is. An end goal is the most important goal you have. Now, do not get an end goal confused with a dream. A dream is merely a thought with no action. An end goal requires action. An end goal is your chief aim. It is the reason you consistently show up to your job during the day and go to school at night. It is the reason you practice or hone your craft daily. It is the reason behind all of your calculated moves. It is what you ultimately hope to achieve by taking certain steps and making certain sacrifices. But before you can actively pursue your end goal, you have to decide what your end goal is. Sometimes all it takes is for you to sit down and think about where you want to be in the next five, ten, or twenty years.

During my childhood, I sat in an assembly listening to a guest speaker. He was rambling on about several things. I say rambling because I was not paying much attention. However, he did get my attention when he asked everyone to raise their hands and state what they wanted to be when they grow up. He motioned to several other children, and they said with confidence what they wanted to be. He then looked in my direction. I intentionally did not make eye contact for two reasons: I was extremely shy at this point in my life, and I was embarrassed to say what I wanted to be. My attempt at avoiding the man was unsuccessful. He pointed directly at me and asked me what I wanted to be. After the assembly, I went home and thought about it long and hard (well, as long as a kid could think about one thing without getting distracted). When I finished thinking, there was no doubt I knew what I wanted.

I wish I could say it will always be that simple, but I cannot. It is quite possible you are complacent. Hence, you are comfortable with where you are right now, and you are not really concerned with what's next. If this is where you are, it may take a life changing experience for you to identify your end goal — similar to the one below.

Approximately five miles outside of Jonestown, Mississippi was a place called HM Haney's Plantation. The late fall months were cold there, especially to an eleven-year-old boy. For the majority of his childhood, he recalls waking up in the wee hours of the morning to pick cotton. Often, it took precedent over going to school. Depending on the financial need of his parents or the need of the owner of the plantation, he and his siblings would often miss school the first semester.

On or about November of 1956, early one morning, his life changed forever. That morning, like most, there were three generations in the cotton field — his grandmother, who was sixty plus, his parents, and his siblings. It was a typical fall morning. In his left hand, was a molasses bucket used to transport a "portable fire"[26] so he could keep warm and on his back was his cotton sack. He used his right hand to pick cotton. As he made his way through the cotton field, he was picking cotton and throwing it in his sack at a rapid pace.

Suddenly, he heard a loud roar coming from his father. He looked toward his father and saw his father running his direction. His father screamed, "Boy don't you know you on fire." The eleven-year-old boy did not realize he was on fire. Nevertheless, after hearing this, he was too scared to move. Before the fire could do any real damage, his father reached him, ripped off the cotton sack and his coat, and then made sure he was okay. It was at that moment, the eleven-year-old boy knew he wanted to get off the plantation so he would never have to pick cotton again. Although the eleven-year-old boy knew he never wanted to pick cotton again, his end goal was not specific and concrete; knowing what you want requires both. Eventually, the eleven-year-old boy understood that.

Similar to the eleven-year-old boy, you too must know what is not for you. Hopefully, it does not take a cold fall morning, cotton picking, and fire to push you in the right direction. However, heading in the right direction does not necessarily mean you have identified your end goal. This may take some time. That time consists of deliberation, discussion, and research. To be as thorough as possible, let's discuss each separately.

---

[26] The fire was made from dried cotton stalks. The cotton pickers would carry matches to set the dried cotton stalks on fire in the molasses bucket.

Deliberation. Close your eyes for a moment. When you think of deliberation, what comes to mind? What do you see? I visualized an older person sitting in a rocking chair sipping on tea just before the sun rises. For those of you who do not have a rocking chair or like drinking tea, you are in luck. Deliberation does not require either. What deliberation does require is careful thought. Hence, spontaneous decisions do not meet the criteria. You must spend time thinking about or contemplating what you want and where you want to be. This greatly reduces the likelihood of backtracking, which is usually associated with arbitrary decisions.

Prior to law school, I spent several weeks thinking about what I wanted out of life and the steps I would have to take to achieve my goal. This trend continued after being accepted into law school. After I had come up with a few short-term goals for myself, I wrote them down. I read over my list of goals every day for the first two weeks of classes and weekly thereafter. This was a very effective way for me to commit to memory and constantly remind myself how important it was to work toward accomplishing my goals and avoiding complacency. Because the list provided a constant reminder, I spent countless hours contemplating on ways to make my dream a reality. This is the type of deliberation needed.

Discussion. Broadcasting your potential goal(s) with reckless abandon is never a good idea. Perhaps, it falls on deaf ears. It is equally as likely that someone who is intentionally working against you gets word of your goal(s) and uses it to his or her advantage. There is a saying that goes, "Don't tell your goals to anyone." That is only partially true. The saying should be, "Don't tell your goals to everyone." It is perfectly fine to discuss your potential plans with the select group of individuals[27] in your life who legitimately have your best interest at heart. Not only is it perfectly fine, but it should also be seriously considered. Discussing your potential goal(s) with the select group gives you the opportunity to get feedback from those who want to see you succeed. Those individuals will likely have different perspectives, which is beneficial when attempting to assess your goal(s).

Research. Yes, research. It is imperative that you spend an adequate amount of time researching your potential goal(s) and ways to achieve such. Reading is an excellent way to begin your research. It gives you a better understanding and lays the foundation for the rest of your research. After you have done the preliminary reading, it is advisable you contact someone in the field who has already traveled the path you are contemplating. For example, if you are considering pharmacy school, it is wise to reach out to a pharmacist or someone who is currently enrolled in a PharmD program. Likewise, if you are thinking about starting your own business, contact someone who has started a successful business. Get as much information from that individual as possible. Essentially, pick his or her brain. Do the same with

---

[27] Make sure your select group have been vetted. These people are your circle of influence.

someone who has failed in that area as well. Your research does not stop here. Continue gathering as much information as possible, which will enable you to make an informed decision when setting a goal.

When you have finished deliberating, discussing, and researching, your goal should be specific and concrete. If it is not, revisit the above principles. For some, it may require much more effort. If you fall into this category, the next step for you is to try your hand at several different things until you reach the point of clarity — knowing what you want. That is exactly what the eleven-year-old boy did.

After the eleven-year-old boy decided cotton-picking would not be part of his future, he began moving in the right direction. He continued to pick cotton during his childhood because it was a necessity. However, during the nights while the rest of his family was sleeping, he laid awake dreaming of a better life for himself. At some point, he decided that education would be his way out. Here lies the conundrum — how could he get an education when attending school was not at the top of the priority list for his family?

These were truly difficult waters for the eleven-year-old boy to navigate. He decided on the days he was required to miss school, instead of lying awake at night dreaming of a better future, he would use the moonlight to see so that he could school himself. As the years went by, the eleven-year-old boy continued to study, which led to him graduating high school at the age of seventeen. After graduation, his father expected him to return to the fields and continue to pick cotton. The boy had other plans. Against his father's wishes, he moved to Chicago where the job opportunities for African-Americans included things other than picking cotton. His plan was to save enough money to go to college.

After a couple of years up north and working several odd jobs, he was able to save enough to begin his college career. He decided to attend Delta State University, which is located in Mississippi, to be closer to his family. Four years later, he graduated with a bachelor's degree. Shortly thereafter, he was drafted to fight in the Vietnam War. After serving in the Army, he was ready to begin his professional career, which proved to be difficult because he was uncertain about what he wanted to do. He decided to go back to school to get his master's degree during the day and work as a machinist manufacturing car parts at night.

During this time, he spent a significant amount of time contemplating and researching different careers. Eventually, he decided to try them all. One of the first jobs of his professional career was as a Job Developer-Interviewer at Mississippi Employment Security Commission in Coahoma County. After he decided to move on, he went through a litany of jobs with different companies including: Fence Installer, Counseling Coordinator with Youth Services (Memphis-USA), Tennessee Army National Guard Reservist, Drug and Alcohol Counselor, Teacher at Coahoma Agricultural High School, Truck Driver for Wonder Bread in Memphis, TN, and Counselor Coordinator with Comprehensive

Employment Training Agency (CETA) in Memphis. He also became an entrepreneur by starting three distinct companies: Love Charms Incorporated, which sold costume jewelry, a moving service, and he bought some rental properties.

Despite being able to secure employment or create opportunities to work, he had yet to find anything he wanted to do long term. Eventually, he got word of an opportunity at Memphis Military Entrancing Processing Station (Memphis MEPS), which is a part of the United States Department of Defense. Memphis MEPS was seeking a Program Manager for the Armed Services Vocational Aptitude Battery (ASVAB). Before he applied, he thought to himself, "Why not?" Ultimately, he was hired. He fell in love with the position. He was able to travel, meet new people, and the part he liked most was the fact it challenged him mentally. Needless to say, he wanted to stay in the position long-term. He finally formed an end goal, retiring as the ASVAB Program Manger, and he did just that after 29 years of service. The boy, turned man, in the story is JB Smiley Sr., my father.

I learned several different things by watching my father and listening to stories about his past. I learned from his successful ventures as well as his failures. Two of the things I learned resonated more than the others. I learned the advantages of knowing what you want. I learned that setting broad or general goals could lead to taking steps in several different directions, but ultimately never leading anywhere. For example, think of an individual stating he wants to be successful. The question that should follow is,

"Successful in what?" You should continue asking specific questions until you are able to narrow down your goal. Once this is done, you are well on your way.

A Narrow Road

When my grandmother, Eloise Coleman, was alive, she would always talk about the Bible and how it is the ultimate guide for our lives. She would tell us to refer to the Bible whenever we need clarity on any subject because any answer we sought would be revealed with prayer and scripture. Hence, it does not surprise me that the Bible also speaks on the dangers of being too broad. The Bible proclaims, "Enter through the narrow gate. For wide is the gate and broad is the road that leads to destruction, and many enter through it. But small is the gate and narrow the road that leads to life, and only a few find it."[28] Find your narrow road, and walk it confidently knowing it is leading to your end goal.

In Chapter 3, I stated the most influential people in my life were my mother, father, and my brother closest to me in age. In this book, I use stories of my life and those individuals who affected it, one way or another, to illuminate certain principles. What I have not discussed is the narrow road my mother traveled to get to her end goal. This is the perfect place to do so.

My mother was born and raised in inner-city Memphis, Tennessee, specifically the Fowler Homes Housing Projects. Some would characterize this area as the "hood", the "ghetto", or simply the "projects." My mother

---

[28] Matthew 7:13-14.

just called it home. The majority of the families who lived there were recipients of welfare.[29] My mother's family was no different. It was her, her mother, and seven siblings all under one roof. I am not sure when my mother realized how poor they were, but they were less financially stable than others in the area. People who grew up in the same area, who were financially dependent on welfare programs as well, would tease them about their financial status or lack thereof. For the most part, their hand-me-down clothes were subject of ridicule. As my mother would say, she was not born with a silver spoon in her mouth.

On one particular day, my grandmother returned home from the food stamp office. As she entered the door, she had a look of utter shock on her face. My mother was puzzled by my grandmother's appearance. Before my mother could say anything, my grandmother exclaimed, "There was a black woman working there!" This was shocking news because this was during the time when Black/African American people in Memphis did not hold those types of jobs. By those, I mean any job that required a college degree. There were a few here or there that had meaningful jobs but none as a welfare (social) worker, at least to my grandmother's knowledge. Because of how amazed my grandmother was by the black woman working in the office as a welfare worker, my mother decided at that moment she wanted to be a social worker. At that time, she did not make her vision or her end goal

---

[29] In this context, generally speaking, Welfare refers to programs funded by taxpayers offered by various government entities that give support to families who are in need.

known. However, down the line she did. Boy, did she regret it.

When my mother began telling people she aspired to be a social worker, the adults did everything but laugh. Although the adults suppressed their laughter, some made it obvious how they felt, especially, one particular family member. She was told people like her do not go to college, but they repeat the cycle of poverty. On one occasion, a family friend called her "a poverty-stricken broad." This hurt my mother to the core. In addition to being extremely poor, her performance in the classroom was lackluster. At this point, she stopped telling people what she aspired to be. However, this did not stop her family member from teasing her. Being teased is one thing, but my mother had a more serious concern.

No one really knew of my mother's struggles in the classroom. Her ability to read and comprehend was limited. My mother practiced and practiced, but she was still not making any significant progress. She went so far as to lock herself in the bathroom at home so she could practice reading aloud. However, her improvement was only minimal. She then tried asking her younger sister to help her with reading but to no avail. She spent years crying because she struggled reading with only minimal improvement. Although she continued to move on to the next grade, her difficulties with reading and comprehending remained.

After she managed to graduate from high school, she decided to attend a two-year college. After enrolling, she took a placement test to determine her strengths and weaknesses. The test revealed she needed several remedial courses, specifically in reading comprehension. As such, she took all the recommended remedial courses. She did everything she could to hide the fact that she was taking remedial courses from her family. She wanted her family to be proud of her, but she did not want them to know about her continued struggles. Her struggles did not deter her; her only focus was her end goal. Although she was on the path to achieving her end goal, she knew from years past that everyone could not see her vision.

Everyone Cannot See

"Success that others see often begins with a vision that only you can see." – Vincent Ivan Phipps

Identifying an end goal is an onerous experience. This end goal or vision is your baby, and you alone will have to nurture it unless you can find others willing to help. Because of this, I believe it is important to discuss the harsh reality of identifying an end goal or vision; everyone will not see it, nor believe it, and it is possible that some may encourage you to abandon it. This presents an interesting question: what do you do when you have "vision" and those around you cannot see? Embrace the responsibility and shed light; well, at least if you find it necessary for them to see. Let me be the first to tell you; if your vision is an extrinsic one, meaning a vision for something outside of oneself, it will require you to shed light on at least one person.

Generally speaking, a person cannot see without light. Likewise, a person cannot see or support your vision if he or she is in the dark. Let me pause for a moment, and say this, do not get shedding light confused with telling all of your plans to someone. Shedding light does not require that. Shedding light is simply getting someone else to believe and support your end goal. Like everything else that has been discussed in this book, you will have to be proactive when shedding light.

Think about it; a person cannot see your vision if you do nothing. With that being said, shedding light presents its own challenges, both internal and external. Without regard for the challenges associated with shedding light, your job is to convince someone your end goal is feasible and should be attained. This is easier said than done, especially if the person does not know you. However, I have done my best to simplify the shedding light process into four steps: 1) Disclosure, 2) Who shall see, 3) Tell them, 4) You told them, now show them.

Disclosure. The first step in this process is determining what information you are comfortable disclosing. You have to decide if disclosing the entire vision would be beneficial. It is quite possible you would be better off disclosing your vision in parts. By revealing parts of your vision, which are your short-term goals, at designated times, you eliminate some of the doubts others may have due to the fact that short-term goals are more feasible, and it takes less time to accomplish. Basically, people have difficulty seeing things further down the road and less trouble seeing those things that are closer. Regardless, it may be better to convey your vision to someone who is in a position to help so that he or she can better understand your short-term goals and assist you along the way. Ultimately, you have to choose what information you are comfortable disclosing. After deciding, move on to the next step—determining who shall see.

Who shall see. The next step is to decide who should take part in your vision. The people you consider can be put into two categories, essential and nonessential. The essential category consists of only those individuals necessary to or who can play a vital role in the fulfillment of your vision. For example, if your vision is to start your own business but you lack cash to do so, you will likely seek a business loan. The loan officer or the person in charge of issuing a loan would fall into the essential category because in order to realize your vision, help from the loan officer is necessary. If a person falls into the essential category, it would be detrimental or impede your progress if you do not disclose. As such, when it comes to the essential category, think inclusion as opposed to exclusion.

Conversely, persons you choose to disclose your vision to but are not essential to the process fall into the nonessential category. The nonessential category usually consists of family, friends, associates, and others. We seek to include them in our plans for various reasons, ranging from encouragement to simply keeping them apprised of what is going on in our lives. Be cautious when shedding light on nonessential persons. Similar to when you began discussing your potential goals, only shed light on the nonessential individuals who truly have your best interest at heart.

Tell them. It is time to communicate your vision with those individuals you have chosen. When you communicate your vision or short-term goals, make sure it is apparent how serious you are about what you have communicated. Make your commitment known. People are more willing to help when it is evident you believe in and are committed to your goals.

My mother, unknowingly, followed each of the above steps. While on her narrow path, which she hoped would lead to the realization of her vision, she had to decide whether it would be beneficial disclosing her entire vision with others, or would she be better suited only relaying her short-term goals. Before deciding, she could not help but think back to her days as a youth when her family member told her it was impossible for her to accomplish such a feat. She did not want to make the same mistake and disclose any information about her short-term or long-term goals with those individuals who would discourage her. She was particularly careful when discussing her vision. She decided that she would only disclose her short-term goals with three people. My mother disclosed her short-term goals to her father because he was essential. He could give her a place to stay while attending college. She also disclosed her short-term goals with nonessential persons as well, her mother and grandfather, because she wanted to make them proud, and she knew they would provide encouragement. My mother made sure each of them knew she was committed to her goals.

The final step, **you told them, now show them.** The last step is to put those words into action. It is nice being able to articulate your goals in such a way people will understand your goals and see your commitment to the same. However, if all you do is talk, those individuals who put faith in you will begin to doubt. Action is not only a prerequisite for shedding light; it is an essential component of it as well. Good thing for my mother, she was much more than talk.

After making her way through and graduating from the two-year college, my mother knew what was next—a four-year university. She had completed her short-term goals and was closer than ever to seeing her vision come to fruition. Notably, during her time at the two-year college, she was not required to declare a major. However, when she began taking classes at the four-year university, declaring a major by her junior year was a must. My mother was backed into a corner because she could not avoid the inevitable any longer. She knew that once she declared a major, most people would either know, figure out, or get wind of what she wanted to do after college. Her vision or end-goal would no longer be a secret.

After declaring a major, she decided to inform the same people she told about her short-term goals about her vision, her end-goal. She told them after college she would become a social worker. All three of them were extremely happy for her. The next two years she received more calls and words of encouragement than prior years. They wanted to make sure they did everything they could to keep my mother motivated. She valued the love and support sent her way.

The closer she became to completing her coursework at the four-year university and receiving her bachelor's degree, the more confident she became that she would reach her end-goal. Ultimately, my mother graduated with her bachelor's degree and went on to pursue her master's. During that time, she worked as a social worker. Much is missing from this story; look to Chapter 7 to find out more.

My mother and father grew up completely different. My mother, a city girl from the "projects," and my father, a country boy from the cotton fields of Mississippi, but they were similar in the sense that both of them could eventually say with confidence, "I know what I want."

They are not alone because you too will be joining them and countless others who have said the magic words, "I know what I want." Let the principles in this chapter— *deliberation, discussion,* and *research,* and also the four steps to shedding light, in addition to the stories that illuminate them serve as your guide when you decide what you want and begin to walk down your narrow road. Remember, the process of identifying your end goal should not be rushed. Rushing often leads to missteps and mistakes. Take it one-step at a time, and learn as much as possible every step. Your time is coming.

Chapter 6

Focus on What You Want

"Obstacles are things a person sees when he takes his eyes off his goal." –E. Joseph Cossman

Knowing what you want is a start. However, the objective is not only to start but also to finish. Finishing or accomplishing a goal is impossible without focus. You can identify your end goal a thousand times and even take steps to accomplish it; if you lose focus, your preliminary efforts will be in vain. Focus shares a symbiotic relationship with commitment. Without focus, we cannot be committed, and without commitment, no goal is within reach. To be successful, developing a focus that is shatterproof or strong enough to withstand both the expected and unexpected happenings of life is a must. Remember, if you focus on the road ahead, you are less likely to stumble.

Focus

"Focusing on what you want" is making your end goal a priority. This is usually extremely difficult largely because life happens! And there is absolutely nothing you can do about it. Inevitability at its finest. Life is full of disappointments, heartaches, trials, and tribulations. All of these things can cause you to lose focus. The average person, in his or her lifetime, experiences unexpected personal illness, the failing health of a loved one, unexpected death of a loved one, career changes, unplanned pregnancy, financial setbacks, relationships problems, and, of course, negative people. These sudden changes have the power to derail your journey toward your goals if your focus is not deeply rooted. What is ironic is that most people will not blame you; some will even make excuses for you. With that in mind, here is a reality check; the strength of your focus is all about you. Your focus is your responsibility. You have to focus and remain focused no matter the circumstances. As the old saying goes, "Keep your eye on the prize..." even when life happens.

My first year of law school is a prime example of life happens. I had to do several things that year—learn how to be a law student, become acclimated to a new city, make new friends, remain in touch with my old friends, transition from an athlete to a business professional,[30] completely change my wardrobe, and do my best to make good grades. On top of that, I began to accumulate debt and did not have a job to lighten the financial burden. If I was going to accomplish anything, I had to focus. At first, I had no problem doing so. Then, life happened!

For the most part, my family would call and check to see how I was doing. At some point, I started to receive fewer calls. I did not notice it at first because I was consumed with all of the things I had going on in my life. Then, my mother's calls became less frequent. I found this peculiar because I received at least one call from her practically every day. I began to call my mother and the rest of my family in Memphis. Most of them would answer

---

[30] This transition was a difficult one for me.

the phone, but when I asked how everyone was doing, I would never get a direct answer. They found several different ways to get me off the phone or to avoid answering the question.

Eventually, my mother told me my uncle was in the hospital. I was told not to worry, he would be fine, and our family was supporting him. At that moment, I should have put "two and two" together, but I did not. In hindsight, the fact that most of my family was frequenting the hospital should have been an indicator his condition was more serious than described. I would call and ask how he was doing and then go on about my day. One night, I called my mother and asked about my uncle like I had done the previous two weeks. This time, she was noticeably upset and could not say much. So I repeated the question. She eventually gained her composure and said, "He is not doing well; you need to go see him."

What do you do when life happens? You deal with each situation as it comes while keeping your eye on your end goal. This does not mean that you should ignore the situation. Most of the time, when life happens, it is impossible to ignore because that situation or incident requires immediate action. Do not run from it, but give each situation the requisite amount of attention to remedy or adequately address it. This may require taking some time to adjust mentally to what has occurred or showing up to support a loved one who is in need. It may require both, but it is essential to your short-term and long-term success that you do not lose sight of what you were focusing on prior to life happening.

When my mother and I ended the call, I sat motionless for a moment trying to think about what I should do next. After all, I had class in the morning, and I still needed to prepare by reading sixty pages of old court opinions full of outdated legal terms that I did not fully understand. Needless to say, I was not as prepared for class as I had been in the past. During class, my mind drifted from the legal reasoning behind certain court decisions to leaving class to visit my uncle. Sometime during the day, it was brought to my attention that in my Property Law class there was a midterm the following week, which I believe was thirty percent of our grade. I did not attend class Friday of that week. Instead, I filled my car up and hit the road toward Memphis. Also, with me were my study materials for the Property Law midterm.

During the two-hour drive to Memphis, all I could think about was my uncle. After driving what seemed to be significantly longer than usual, I finally arrived in Memphis. Immediately after crossing the bridge, I went straight to the hospital. When I entered the waiting room, my cousin greeted me. Her eyes were full of tears. While fighting back tears of my own, I asked the magic words, "Can I see him?" I was taken to his room. As I entered, I laid my eyes on a person who did not resemble my uncle at all. The person lying in the hospital bed had his leg amputated, and he was practically skin and bones. I could not deny the fact that the man lying in the hospital bed was indeed my uncle. I could not handle seeing him in such a fragile state. I rushed out of the hospital room and went into the waiting area. All I could think about was my uncle; I could not even pretend to be strong. I left the hospital in an attempt to come to grips with what the doctors said would be sure to come, his impending death.

While I was home, the only break I got from the days full of sorrow was my time spent studying for the Property midterm. My ability to focus on my goal, passing the Property midterm, seemed to be my only outlet. When it was time for me to leave, I visited the hospital one last time. I went into his room and saw the same frail and semi-conscious man as before. I wanted to say so much, but the only thing I could think of was, I will do this for you. What I meant was, I am going to do well for you.

Sometime during the next couple of weeks, the results of my Property midterm came in, I exceeded my own expectations. Also to the doctors' complete surprise, my uncle improved dramatically. He continued to improve such that he could hold full conversations again. During the course of his improvement, I returned home and visited the hospital once more. This time, he was completely conscious and knew it was me. The first thing he asked me was, "Were we still going to have a lawyer in the family? With a smile on my face, I responded, "No doubt, Unc!"

If a storm is approaching and life is getting ready to happen, brace yourself. The first step you should take is to gather your wits, and force your focus into overdrive. Roy T. Bennett said it best in his book, The Light in the Heart, "Focus on your goals, not your fear." Hold on to your goal and whatever you do, do not let go. This will make the storm more bearable. It will give you a temporary safe haven in the midst of the calamity, and you will survive the storm in your life without losing focus.

Helpful Hints for Staying Focused

Look at it this way. Focusing is the vehicle that enables you to get from Point A to Point B; you cannot get to your destination without it. As such, coming up with a strategy to reduce the likelihood of losing focus would be beneficial. Below, I have identified seven strategies or techniques to help you keep your focus. I have personally tested these strategies and have witnessed them work for others.

Surround yourself with like-minded individuals. I heard a song that goes, "You got people that surround you. They gone try their best to down you. Keep them squares up out your circle."[31] This song suggests that you should cease to socialize with or allow individuals in your life who do not add positive and productive energy to your circle of influence. Instead, surround yourself with focused and motivated individuals; people who are driven, like you.

By surrounding yourself with a team of like-minded individuals, you reduce the negativity in your life and create a more positive environment, which allows you to flourish. This will assist you in maintaining an unbreakable focus. For those of you like me, seeing others succeed only increases your drive and focus on doing the same. So, don't forget, "Keep them squares out of your circle," and add like-minded individuals.

---

[31] Rocko, *Squares Out of Your Circle.*

108

Write it down. If you are like me, you are probably thinking to yourself there is no need to write your goal(s) down because you already know the things you want to accomplish. Wrong! Research indicates those who write their goals down achieve their goals at a significantly higher percentage than those who do not write their goals down.[32] In a study conducted by Dr. Matthews, 267 participants were recruited from a variety of different businesses and backgrounds throughout the United States and other countries for a study on how goal achievement in the workplace is influenced by writing goals, committing to goal-directed actions, and accountability for those actions.[33] Notably, only 149 of those recruited completed the study. The participants ranged in age from 23 to 72.[34]

The participants were divided into five distinct groups.[35] Group 1 consisted of those participants who only

---

[32] Dr. Gail Matthews, Dominican University, *Goals Research Summary*, available at
http://www.dominican.edu/academics/ahss/undergraduate-programs/psych/faculty/assets-gail-matthews/researchsummary2.pdf.

[33] STUDY FOCUSES ON STRATEGIES FOR ACHIEVING GOALS, RESOLUTIONS,
http://www.dominican.edu/dominicannews/study-highlights-strategies-for-achieving-goals.

[34] *Id.*

[35] Dr. Gail Matthews, Dominican University, *Goals Research Summary*, available at
http://www.dominican.edu/academics/ahss/undergraduate-

thought about their goals but did not write them down.[36] Group 2 was asked to write their goals into an online survey.[37] Group 3 was asked to write their goals into the online survey and also formulate an action commitment.[38] Group 4 was asked to write their goals into an online survey, formulate an action commitment, and send their goals and action commitment to a supportive friend.[39] Group 5 was asked to write their goals into the online survey, formulate action commitments and send their goals, action commitments, and weekly progress reports to a supportive friend.[40]

After four weeks, the participants reported their progress. The results were astonishing. Group 1, those who merely thought about their goals, achieved their goals at a rate of about 43 percent but the mean of Group 2-5, those who had at least written their goals down, achieved at a rate of 64 percent.[41] Additionally, Group 2 also outpaced Group 1, 61 percent to 43 percent.[42] Notably, the

---

programs/psych/faculty/assets-gail-matthews/researchsummary2.pdf.

[36] *Id.*

[37] *Id.*

[38] *Id.*

[39] *Id.*

[40] *Id.*

[41] *Supra* Matthews, Goal Research Summary.

participants in Group 5, those who sent weekly progress reports to their friend, *accomplished significantly more* than those who had unwritten goals, wrote their goals, formulated action commitments or sent those action commitments to a friend.[43] Group 5 achieved at a rate of 76 percent.[44]

As you can see, the advantages of writing you goals down are apparent. Those who do, achieve at a significantly higher rate than those who do not. You may want to consider formulating and writing down an action plan in addition to writing weekly progress reports to hold yourself accountable. This will only increase your focus. Do yourself a favor; write your goals down.

Do not worry about things out of your control. You will encounter numerous situations throughout your life where you have absolutely no control. That is just a part of it, and that is okay. You have to learn to accept and move on from the need to control everything. We are not omnipotent beings.

However, you do have the power to control some things. You can control how much you study for an upcoming test or exam. You can control how you respond to someone's remarks, whether good or bad. You can control whether you will remain complacent or begin to actively pursue your goals. You can control the amount of effort you put in endeavors in which you partake. Direct

---

[42] *Id.*

[43] *Id.*

[44] *Id.*

your attention to the things you can control. This will have an impact on much of what happens in your life, effectively giving you the control you seek.

Do not spread yourself too thin. I have a confession. This principle was the most difficult for me. For most of my life, I had a severe case of the "cant-say-no's." As such, I often found myself agreeing to do or assist with several projects. Because of this illness, I struggled finding time to devote to the most pressing matters in my life. Do not allow this to happen to you. There is nothing wrong with saying no. In fact, it will be required when you begin to focus.

Spreading yourself too thin also includes setting too many goals and attempting to pursue them all at once. Once again I am guilty. A very knowledgeable person once told me that there is no such thing as multitasking; there is only unproductive task shifting. Because that is what happens when you are attempting to pursue or accomplish too many goals at once, you should focus on the most pressing goal. Give yourself an adequate amount of time to correct any missteps along the way. Take it one step at a time, one goal at a time.

Reduce distractions. If what you are attempting or beginning to focus on is a goal of yours, nothing less than your best is sufficient. You cannot focus if you are distracted — simple as that. You should not attempt to begin a goal if you are distracted because it usually leads to a less than stellar product. Reduce distractions at all costs. It will be worth it in the end.

To avoid a subpar effort caused by a lack of focus, take an in-depth look at your life. Pay particular attention to those things that cause you to lose focus. Next, you must decide if the distraction is avoidable or unavoidable. After determining which distractions can be avoided, remove those distractions from your life. By doing this, you will be in prime position to focus on what is important, accomplishing your goal.

Affirmation. Simply put, this principle is speaking your goals into existence. Relax, this does not require any type of voodoo, black magic, or supernatural power. What is required is speaking with authority. As my former law professor, Terrance Cain, would say, "Put some base in your voice." Tell yourself you will accomplish your goals. Do this consistently and as often as possible.

Eventually, if you did not believe before, you will begin to believe. Once you believe, you will take concerted efforts toward the fulfillment of whatever goal you have set. Do not limit affirmation to yourself; have those individuals in your circle of influence call and tell you that you will reach your goal as well. This further instills in you confidence in your ability to achieve your goal. Your response to those calls is a simple one, and I cannot put it any better than my friend Mrs. Jasmine Samarco, "I receive that." By saying "I receive that" in response, you are essentially confirming the affirmation and telling the person and yourself, you believe it to be true. With affirmation, you are speaking life into your dreams, goals, and aspirations.

The mental game. The mental game requires you to challenge yourself by setting certain markers or milestones within your goal and then rewarding yourself after the marker is reached. However, if you fail to reach the marker within the time constraints you have set, you withhold the reward, effectively punishing yourself. This gives you an added incentive to focus and hopefully accomplish your goal.

For example, if you were to set a goal to lose 12lbs in three weeks, the potential marker could be every 4lbs lost. Once you have reached a marker, you could reward yourself by buying a nice shirt or treating yourself to a spa day, etc., gradually improving the reward until you have achieved your goal. If you have a significant other or friend, you can include him or her in the reward aspect. I have found this principle to be most effective for me. This does not mean that *the mental game* will be the most effective for you; some of the other techniques may prove more helpful. Figure out which technique(s) works best for you and stick with it.

Lost Focus

All of the previous pages of this chapter have been about focusing and for good reason. Because when it comes to maximizing your potential, there is nothing more important than focusing. Then again, focusing is not a simple process. It is much easier to say you are focused and will remain focus than it is actually to do so. As such, it is understood not everyone will stay the course, and some will lose focus.

What happens if you lose focus? Do you just pick back up where you left off? Will you get a second chance to accomplish your goal? Will society write you off? Will others laugh when it appears that you have fallen short? Do you have to start from the beginning? Will you have to set new goals? I prefer to give yes or no answers, but there is no way around it; the answer to all of the questions is, it depends. It depends on several factors: 1) How big of a mistake you have made; 2) Are there any stigmas associated with your mistake; 3) How long were you unfocused; and 4) How much time has passed since you pursued your goal? Someone very close to me had to answer those very questions because he lost focus.

During my high school years, he and I shared some of the same hobbies. The one that brought us closer together than any of the others was basketball. I recall multiple conversations where he would tell me he was going D-1. For those of you who are unfamiliar with sports' lingo, D-1 means NCAA Division I. D-1 is the most highly regarded of the collegiate basketball associations. It goes without saying, his goal was a lofty one. The fact that the odds were not in his favor did not deter him from pursuing his goal with all that was in him. At this point in his life, he epitomized what it meant to focus.

There were many naysayers, but he stayed the course. In the words of Drake, they were not with him shooting in the gym. Therefore, they did not know how hard he worked on his craft. He continued to improve on the basketball court. During his senior year, I watched him score thirty points on the highest ranked player in the state of Tennessee, who was also one of the best players in the nation. He was well on his way to accomplishing his goal.

We spoke often, and we always discussed who was the better basketball player. We had a friendly rivalry in that regard. However, at a point still uncertain to me, he completely lost focus. This was a monumental mistake. By losing focus, he allowed himself to get involved with the wrong crowd. This ultimately led him down a path full of horrible and asinine decisions. This continued until he made the worst decision of his life. I remember getting the call about it.

I was sitting in my living room watching television. I glanced at my cellphone and saw several missed calls. I did not think anything of it, but I did decide to take my phone off silent at that point. Almost simultaneously, my phone rang. I answered it and said, "what's up?" The person on the other end responded, "Smiley have you heard? He is number three on Memphis Most Wanted List." I laughed and told the person to quit playing. Then, there was silence. Abruptly, cutting the silence short, the person said he was serious, and I should check the news or call home to find out more. That was only the beginning of the calls. By the end of the day, I received several calls ranging from people being legitimately concerned about him to others just being nosey. Eventually, I was able to verify the validity of what had been reported. Indeed, he was number three on Memphis Most Wanted List. For the rest of the day, I sat in disbelief. I was still in complete shock. I tossed and turned all night asking myself where did he go wrong and how did I let it happen.

The next day, it was impossible for me to concentrate. At some point during the day, I received a call from a number I did not recognize. I answered the call not knowing who was on the other end; it was him. Before I could say a word, he began to talk. He told me that he was calling me from a payphone, and he was sure I got word of his current situation. He stated, "I'm straight. I need to figure something out..." The call ended. He was apprehended not long after.

Within his first two weeks of incarceration, he sent me a letter. In the letter, he explained to me how he lost focus on things that were meaningful. He said he got hooked up with the wrong crowd, which led to him making bad decision after bad decision. I could tell from the letter that he was truly remorseful. However, remorse could not undo his bad decision-making. He ended up serving over nine years in prison. His lost focus, which led to more bad decisions, created a void in the lives of his loved ones. He was not thinking about the repercussions of his actions that were sure to follow because he lost focus.

During his incarceration, he had plenty of time to reflect and to answer the questions I previously mentioned. He knew that his aspirations of playing D-1 had come to an end, and the only place he would showcase his ability to play basketball was prison. He knew a stigma would be attached to his felon status. He knew most of society would write him off. He knew he would have to set new goals and start from the beginning. Although this appears to be a daunting task, he was up for the challenge. However, this time, he knew that staying focus was the key, and he was determined to do just that.

If you could ask him today about the importance of staying focused, he would tell you it is everything. Not only does losing focus affect your life but it has an impact on those around you as well. The repercussions of your lost focus could be the sorrow of your friends and family. Quite possibly, it could be something more concrete. For example, imagine you are on pace to get an academic or athletic scholarship, but you lose focus, and your performance in the classroom or field falters. As a result of your poor performance, the potential scholarship never comes. Because of this, you have to take out multiple loans, which follow you into your marriage. Perhaps, your parents are in a position to help, and they pay for your education. Either way, you have a negative impact on the lives of your spouse or parents because you lost focus. This can all be avoided if you stay the course and never lose focus. But in reality, everyone does not do so.

Refocus

Although negative consequences are a certainty if you lose focus, it is not an end all. If you have air in your lungs, blood in your veins, and a functioning brain, it is possible for you to refocus and bounce back. Think minor setback before a major comeback. Although it is possible to refocus, there are certain steps you must take to do so. See below.

1. <u>Acknowledgment</u>

The first step in the refocusing process (Yes, it is a process) is acknowledging that you are off course. At all times you must be mindful of your chief aim. If you find yourself further from reaching your chief aim than you were at the outset, you lost focus somewhere down the line. A good way to determine if you have lost focus is by keeping a progress log. This allows you to track your progress, find out if you are regressing, or stagnant. If you are any of the latter two, acknowledge the fact that you have lost focus.

Consider the following hypothetical. I hope you remember our friends from the first chapter, Marcus and Josh. Marcus and Josh have now become friends. Because of Marcus' success and encouragement, Josh decided to pursue his master's in business management as well. Josh has successfully completed half of the course work needed to obtain such degree. Lately, he has been given opportunities to work longer hours and make more money. Following the increase in availability of extra hours, Josh decided to take some time off from school to capitalize on the opportunities. Josh's time off became a semester off and then a year.

Marcus noticed Josh not moving in the direction of a person who made it his goal to obtain a master's degree. Marcus suggested that Josh create a progress log, which he was to list all of his goals and keep track of his progress. Josh agreed. After creating a progress log, it became apparent to him that he was no longer on course to obtain his master's degree.

2. Assess the Cause

The second step is to assess the cause. In order for you to get back on track and refocus, you must identify the stumbling block. There are multiple ways you can determine if something has caused or was the cause of your temporary (I sure hope it's temporary) lost of focus. The simplest way for you to figure out where you went wrong is by taking a step back and putting things into proper perspective, which means you look to the beginning. Track your progress from the start until it is evident that your progress has plateaued or taken a nosedive. It will be at this point in which the stumbling block reared its head. Pay particular attention to what is different in your life, including but not limited to actions you are taking, acquaintances, or living situation.

Picking back up with the hypothetical about Josh, when we left he had determined he was no longer on course to obtain his master's degree. Earning his master's degree was important to him; he decided to assess the cause by identifying the stumbling block. He began the assessing process by analyzing where he was at the start of the master's program to where he is now. He noted significant progress during the first half of the program. He realized the only thing different than before was his increased hours at work.

3. Prioritize

Once you have identified the stumbling block, the next step is to prioritize. Please note, if your stumbling block is something that would be considered noise, refer to chapter one of this book, "Turning Off the Noise." If not, rank your goals or current objectives in order of importance. This will give you clarity regarding what matters most—accomplishing your chief aim.

4. Be Intentional

The final step is being intentional to bring about a shift in your focus. Purposefully direct your attention toward your chief aim. Be deliberate! Every thought, action, and interaction should put you in a better position to achieve your goal. Do this until you are back on track and focused. Hopefully, you do not lose focus again, but if you ever find yourself off track once more, repeat the above steps. You got this!

When we last left Josh, he realized that the increased workload was the only thing different from before. The money was good, but he knew he wanted to graduate with a master's. He decided to list all of his goals in the order of importance. After creating a list, he realized how important the master's degree was to him and his future. He was no longer as concerned about the money. He began to contemplate what he needed to do to get back on track and refocus. He decided the best step for him was to be intentional to bring about a shift in his focus. For the next few weeks, Josh made every decision with the master's degree in mind. His hours were back to normal. He was back in school, and before he knew it, he was no longer plateauing. He was progressing. Josh was refocused.

Similar to Josh's realization that focusing was imperative to the manifestation of his dreams, you too must be cognizant of the importance of focusing. Life will present many distractions, some unavoidable. Do not be deterred. You are capable of focusing even when life happens. If you happen to lose focus, it is not the end of the road for you. You were born with everything you need to refocus and get back on the road to achievement. At the beginning of this chapter, it was stated focusing on what you want is making your end goal a priority. You make your end goal, chief aim, or ultimate objective, or whatever you want to call it a priority by choosing to put it near the top of your list of things you want to accomplish.

What I hope I have accomplished with this chapter is to impress upon you how important it is to focus. If you had the opportunity to talk with my friends, they would tell you I am extremely focused and determined to achieve whatever goal I have set for myself. One goal I have not set is improving my ability to carry a note. I am probably in the top ten of the worst singers you have never had the privilege of hearing. However, if you lose focus, or stumble along the way, I want you to imagine sitting in the car with me while I sing the following lyrics: Every move you make, every step you take, for your sake, should get you closer to your goal.[45]

---

[45] The lyrics are a play off of a song by Sting titled "Every Breath You Take."

Chapter 7

Be Determined

"Whatever we believe about ourselves and our ability comes true for us." –Susan L. Taylor

You know what you want, and you are focused; nothing is stopping you now! You must adopt this mentality before you can truly say you are determined to achieve. Achieving anything of significance requires determination. If accomplishing a goal requires back-to-back all-nighters, you find a way to stay up and get the job done. If getting to where you want to go requires hard work, determination necessitates a willingness to outwork anyone to get there. Even if your current situation is less than ideal, let nothing stand in your way.

In Chapter 5, I discussed, at length, my mother's story and her difficulties reading and comprehending. What I intentionally omitted was why she struggled and how she overcame. My mother hid her shortcomings from her family and friends. However, she could not hide from or escape the reality of her situation. She had to face it head on. Even after she was in her professional field as a social worker, her struggles reading and comprehending made her job more difficult than it needed to be.

One day during a routine visit with one of her clients, the woman began to tell my mother about all of her kids. One child, in particular, stood out. The woman explained some of the difficulties the child was going through. She told my mother her son was extremely bright, but he had trouble reading. She said he hated to read aloud. The woman began to name some of his other problems: difficulty memorizing, comprehending, hearing the similarities and differences in letters, and spelling. As the woman was listing her son's problems, my mother immediately thought of herself. She had almost all of the same problems as the woman's son. Then the woman said a word my mother had not heard before, dyslexia. My mother responded bluntly by saying, "What?!" The woman said her son was recently diagnosed with something called dyslexia.

My mother was able to keep her composure for the rest of the visit, at least that's what she told me. The next several days were full of research and calls to doctors' offices. At the end of her research and inquiries, only one conclusion could be reached; she was dyslexic. My mother was relieved because she finally realized why she struggled for so long.

For the first time in her life, my mother embraced and opened up about her struggles. This discovery did not have the effect one might imagine. My mother's resolve increased exponentially and also her ambition. She decided to pursue her master's degree, something in which she did indeed obtain. Her purpose for pursuing the degree was not solely for personal satisfaction but to set an example. She wanted to motivate others to pursue their goals and to be determined to achieve them even if they happened to be a poor, dyslexic girl from the projects.

When I came of age, my mother told me all about her condition and every symptom that came to mind. For most of my childhood, I never gave much thought to my mother's trials and her ability to persevere despite being in a less than ideal situation. It was not until I was a young adult before I could appreciate the foundation she laid for me. Her past served as a shining example of something that is inside of us all—the ability not to give up, but to fight on. She worked nonstop, which included her "off days,"[46] to achieve her end goal. That is exactly what you must do to achieve yours. On April 1, 2016, I had an opportunity to convey the same sentiments to an individual that I met in passing.

On that day, I traveled from Little Rock to Memphis for my cousin's homegoing celebration. After it had come to an end, and when I finished fellowshipping with my family, I began walking toward my car. As I approached, I noticed a significant amount of dirt on it. I decided to drive to a do-it-yourself carwash. When I arrived, I got out of my car and began taking my floor mats out to dust them off. Before I could finish, a man approached me.

He asked me if he could wash my car or vacuum it out for a few dollars. I told him thanks, but no thanks, I could do it myself. Although I had begun to clean my car, I paid close attention to his interaction with a guy who was driving a miniature tour bus. The man washed the entire tour bus for the guy and was only given one dollar in return. Apparently, the man was watching me too because when I ran out of quarters, which were needed to continue

---

[46] There is no such thing as an off day until you have achieved your end goal.

cleaning my car, he asked me if I needed any change. I told him I did, but I was going to the store to get change. When I returned, the man was still there.

This time, I motioned over to him. I asked him to tell me his story. He complied. I continued to clean my car while he was telling me how he came to be in his current situation. He revealed that he was only a few years older than I, and he was homeless. He told me he was trying to earn enough money to get in the shelter for the day, which costs 7 dollars and fills up quickly. Before I could respond, he said, "Sir, I just don't want to be rained on again." I told him not to worry and then asked him if he was hungry. He nodded his head. I told him I would meet him at the Taco Bell across the street after I finished cleaning my car.

When I arrived at Taco Bell, I looked around and did not see the man anywhere. I stood near the counter awkwardly before asking the cashier if he had seen a homeless guy come in carrying a backpack. After asking the question, I noticed the cashier and the people at the counter waiting for their food looking at me with a puzzled expression. The cashier responded, "Several homeless people come in the restaurant, but none buy food." Although his answer was not responsive to my question, I waited a bit more. The man showed up shortly after that. He looked at me, and I told him to order whatever he liked. One of the customers who previously had a puzzled look on his face glanced at me and said, "Thank you for doing that" as he exited the restaurant.

While he was eating, we began to converse. I asked him what he would do if I paid for his next three days at the shelter. He said he planned on working two of the days and resting on the other. His response sparked something in me. For the first time during our interaction, I told him about my life and how motivated I was to see my goals come to fruition. I explained to him that some people around me say I should rest more because I recently accomplished one of my goals. Once again, he nodded his head in agreement. I smiled and said no; that is not how you get ahead.

At this point, he was fully engaged, which was evidenced by the fact he put down his Chalupa. I told him my response to those individuals is always and will always be the same, "I will sleep when I'm dead." He did not get it so I explained further. I did not literally mean I never sleep, but I do not take any days off because I am always working toward accomplishing a goal I have set. Not knowing if he fully understood what I was trying to say, I went a step further and told him, "You do not have time to take a day off because your goal, getting off the streets and into a stable living situation, is very pressing and urgent. You must work toward it daily." After our conversation, he stated that he has never been so motivated. As we departed, I gave him my card and told him to call me with his progress. He thanked me for it and said, "You are right; there is no time to rest and working toward my goal is now my only focus." I responded, "Indeed, life is hard; you must work harder."

My last statement to the man is what being determined to achieve is all about. If knowing what you want is the bridge, and focusing on what you want is the vehicle, then being determined to achieve is the fuel needed to get across the bridge. Your fuel, which consists of your determination, your drive, and your will to succeed, determines how far you get and how much you accomplish. The good thing about your fuel is no gas station is needed. Likewise, you do not need someone to fill your tank up or any gas money. Your fuel is like renewable energy, naturally occurring and constantly renewing. You are "Born With it." However, it is up to you to use that fuel.

The latter part of my 8th-grade year, I was able to witness what being determined to achieve looks like. I could continue trying to explain it, but that would not do the story justice. Before I tell you what occurred, just know that being determined to achieve is not always pretty, but when you are, it is an unbelievable source of strength.

During my middle school years, I grew closer to one of my cousins and aunts. My cousin and I were born two weeks apart. We attended the same middle school, and we rode the same bus. I was at his house practically every day. It was not strange for his mother, my aunt, to fuss at me as if I was her own son. Fussing was not the only thing she did; she fed me as well. For those of you who do not know me, I am easily won over by home cooked meals. Although she did not have to win me over, she cooked for me because she loved me. The love was mutual.

We all grew closer by the day. We were together frequently enough for my cousin and I to predict how each other would respond in certain situations. The same went for his mother. Every morning that I was there, we could predict her routine. She would yell our names and tell us to get up. She would then proceed into the kitchen to get her coffee started. (Notice, it's her coffee. It did not matter how much we begged and pleaded; we were not getting any of her coffee). If we did not get up, she would come into the room and scream some more. She would finish doing some other miscellaneous tasks until her coffee was ready to be consumed. When her coffee was ready, she would get her mug, pour her coffee into it, and sit at the table until we made our way into the front room. She made sure we had everything we needed, and then we would proceed to the bus stop.

On the days that I had basketball games, although my playing time was limited at best, she was sitting right beside my mother in the stands. I grew accustomed to seeing her and seeing her healthy, but things slowly began to change for the worst. My aunt stopped showing up as often. Because I was a child and did not understand certain things, the reasons were not obvious. In hindsight, it was apparent that her energy level began to decrease. Eventually, she checked herself into the hospital. My cousin was devastated. I pretended to be strong, but I was deeply saddened. I felt like I was losing my mother.

The very first day I visited her in the hospital was surreal. On the way there, I came up with a plan to make her smile because I knew she would be down. I even rehearsed a joke in my mind. I got as mentally prepared as I could before arriving. Once we arrived, I cannot recall what was said on the way to her room. The walk from the car to her hospital room was a blur. When we entered I saw her lying there in a hospital gown. She was hooked up to an IV and an oxygen machine. I could tell she was appreciative for us coming to visit her, although she was too tired to say much. I did not know how severe her condition was, but to my cousin and I it seemed to be dire.

What made the situation more alarming to my cousin and I was the fact that all of the adults were whispering about her condition, attempting to keep us kids in the dark. My cousin and I looked at each other as if hope was lost; we both expected the worst. Several weeks later, she was released. That was when we found out the doctors did not expect her to make it, and she was in the hospital fighting for her life. I was elated she was released. Because she was released and the fact that I was only a child, I assumed she was healthy again. Wrong! She was still in a fight for her life.

Per the doctor's orders, she had to have an oxygen machine on twenty-four hours a day, seven days a week, and lose weight, in addition to taking several medications. By doing all of these things, the doctors still could not guarantee that she would live a long healthy life, but my aunt was determined. She refused to give in. To be blunt, she refused to die. She carried her oxygen machine with her to the gym, sat it beside her treadmill, and exercised. Despite the fact her energy levels were low, and she could only workout for five minutes at a time in the outset, the people at her gym were amazed at her determination and strength. One guy was so inspired when he saw her struggling in the gym but refusing to give up; he stopped working out to speak to and pray for her. Her determination paid off. She continued to get better. Her workout times increased, and her medications decreased. As of today, she does not need an oxygen machine.

When I began writing this chapter, I reflected on all of the obstacles my aunt had overcome to achieve her goal. This ultimately led me to calling her. When I asked her about the entire experience, which occurred many years prior, you could tell from her voice it was all still fresh on her mind. She was hesitant at first, but she eventually began to talk through the entire ordeal. She mentioned how hard she prayed and how much she worked. When I asked her why she kept fighting and why she was so determined, the phone got quiet. I was uncertain if she was still on the phone, but then she spoke. She stated her motivation was her son. She did not want him to grow up without a mother.

My aunt's battle with sickness taught me several lessons, none more important than the other. I witnessed a person winning a battle when those around her doubted her ability to achieve. I learned determination, the will to fight on, is not eroded by sickness, struggle, or doubts of another. It is embedded deep within us all. I learned even when you go through, you must be determined to achieve and fight on! Thankful for that lesson, because that is exactly what I had to do.

Going Through

Approximately three days before opening my laptop and starting on page one of this book, my resolve was tested, and the only way I was going to get through was if I was determined to achieve. But first, you have to know the back-story.

During law school, I always studied with my laptop. I mean everything was on my laptop. My notes were on my laptop. My outlines were on my laptop. Anything that I had ever written was on my laptop. Needless to say, when it was time to take a final exam, when given the option to write out our exam or to type our exam and submit it on a laptop, I chose to use my laptop. For every class that I took that required any form of written assignment or examination, I would use my laptop.

Upon graduation, it was time to start studying for the notorious bar exam. To put myself in the best position to be successful on the most important and difficult exam of my life, I took a bar preparation course. Let me lay the proper foundation for bar preparation courses and all it entails. Bar preparation courses are offered to better prepare a graduating law student for the bar exam. The bar exam preparation courses cost upwards of $2,000 in addition to the fees you pay to the state in which you take the bar exam. When you are done paying fees, a person taking the bar exam and using a preparation course is out of at least $3,000. Okay, back to the story.

The preparation course provided several books on every legal subject imaginable, but as you can see from what I have already told you, I preferred to use my laptop. So it should be no surprise the preparation courses offered an online platform that could be used to study. Of course, the online platform was my primary means of studying for the bar exam. I took the Arkansas Bar Exam first. Before taking the Arkansas Bar Exam, I accepted a position with Munson, Rowlett, Moore, & Boone, P.A., a law firm in Little Rock, Arkansas. It was expected that I would pass the bar exam on the first attempt[47] and begin practicing as a lawyer. The truth of the matter is, everyone taking the bar exam would not pass. The Arkansas Bar Exam was tough, but I was able to manage because I was able to use my laptop for the examination. I passed the Arkansas Bar Exam on the first attempt.

Enough of the backstory, but it is apparent that I relied on my laptop whenever I was required to write anything of significance. I relied on it for a few reasons— my poor penmanship, I could type faster than write, and the ability to edit and make changes on the laptop when a mistake was made without the need to erase. At some point, I had the bright idea to take the Tennessee Bar Exam as well. This is when my life temporarily turned upside down, and my *fuel* had to get me through.

My study habits did not change this time around. I used my laptop to study from November of 2015 up until the day the Tennessee Bar Exam began, February 23, 2016. The exam is a two-day test, lasting eight hours each day,

---

[47] In Arkansas, approximately 30 percent of the first time bar exam takers fail.

covering multiple areas of Tennessee and Federal law. The day before the test I drove to Nashville, Tennessee and found a hotel just a few miles from the testing location. Once I arrived, I checked in and went to Waffle House to grab a bite to eat. I arrived back at my room around 7 o'clock. I did not plan to go anywhere else.

I attempted to watch television, but my mind was on the exam; I decided to study. Not only did I prepare and study in advance, but I also crammed. When I was tired of sitting up and studying, I took my laptop to bed with me to continue studying. Eventually, my eyes gave out, and I could no longer stare at the screen. I got up, took a shower, brushed my teeth, and said a prayer. I was ready and prepared for any legal question that would come my way. Little did I know, answering legal questions would be the least of my worries.

I arrived at the testing location and saw a line of people entering and waiting to be seated for the bar exam. As I walked in the location, I had a sense of confidence. Others were bickering and studying but not me; I was as cool as the other side of the pillow.[48] I even Snapchatted[49] some of my friends while in line waiting to be seated. Eventually, I reached the registration desk. I signed in and went to my seat after dropping off all prohibited items in the area reserved for such.

---

[48] A phrase made popular by the legendary basketball commentator and reporter, Stuart Scott.

[49] Snapchat is a social media app with increasing popularity.

When I went to my assigned seat, I only had a few things with me—pens, earplugs, my license, my eyeglasses, and the most important item of all, my laptop. As I scanned the room, I saw nervous faces everywhere. There were several proctors in the room as well. The head proctor announced the exams were being passed out and that we were not to open them until instructed to do so. Once we received the exam, the head proctor began giving detailed instructions regarding every situation or matter imaginable, from how to proceed if you have to use the restroom to what will happen if you continue to work when the time is called. One of the things he discussed was what to do in case your laptop crashes during the examination. I was not completely listening at this point, but I do recall him saying raise your hand and put up a certain amount of fingers. Although, I believed this procedure applied in the case of a laptop failure, I was not particularly concerned because I had never had any issues with my laptop before.

Shortly after that, the head proctor gave the only instruction that mattered to me, "You may begin!" I quickly opened up the booklet and started reading the question at hand. This part of the examination was called the Multi-State Performance Test, known by law students and lawyers alike as the infamous MPT.[50] I had approximately 90 minutes to complete this section. After reading and determining how I wanted to approach

---

[50] You can find out more about the MPT at the National Conference of Bar Examiners website, http://www.ncbex.org/exams/mpt/preparing.

answering the question, I began to type at a brisk pace. I am not sure where the time went, but the head proctor announced there was only 30 minutes remaining. When the announcement was made, I immediately determined I needed all 30 minutes to finish.

I continued to type and read over my legal analysis. After 15 minutes had gone by, I decided to delete a large portion of my notes, which were typed below my actual answer to the MPT. I highlighted all of my notes and then hit delete, but nothing happened. I waited for a moment to see if anything would change. Indeed, something did change; the thinking icon appeared on the screen. I calmly sat there for a minute thinking the issue would resolve itself. Another minute or so went by, and I raised my hand frantically motioning for the on-site tech staff to come and fix my computer. Time was ticking.

Three minutes had gone by before a tech person came to assist me. He stared at my laptop, hit a button or two, and then told me he needed to get his supervisor. Several more minutes went by before the supervisor arrived. My laptop was still frozen. Before I knew it, time was called. I was told I would not be given extra time to complete the MPT and whatever was on my computer a minute prior to it freezing would be graded. I was bothered at this point but not too concern because the supervisor told me they would get my laptop working during the 10-minute break. After all, I still had nine essays to type that day.

During the break, I was instructed to raise my hand prior to the start of the exam so that a proctor could bring me a bluebook, which was used by those individuals writing the essays as opposed to typing, if my laptop could not be repaired. I assumed the proctor who informed me was wasting his breath because the tech support supervisor told me he would have my laptop up and running before the essay portion began. I sat patiently waiting for the tech supervisor to fix my laptop. While doing so, the head proctor made the announcement for us to begin the essays. The tech support supervisor was still working on my laptop two minutes into the essay portion. I concluded that my laptop would not be fixed, and I had to begin writing an examination for the first time since August of 2012, when I started law school.

I abruptly raised and waved my hand (I am pretty sure this was not the appropriate procedure, but I needed a bluebook immediately). There were three essays to write before the next break. The time went by extremely slow. Prior to writing a single word, negative thoughts were creeping in. Also, the tech supervisor and the other tech support staff were standing directly to my left working on my laptop. I attempted to block them out, but they would not let me. While I was reading and trying to answer the essay questions, the tech support continued to interrupt me asking if I could log into my computer after they had restarted it several times. I politely asked them, well as politely as imaginable under the circumstances, to take my laptop and let me be. I also wrote the password down for them.

Negative thoughts plagued me for the entire 90 minutes. The thoughts ranged from the graders inability to read my writing to I did not have enough time to actually write an answer adequately addressing each issue raised in the essay questions. Finally, time was called. I felt defeated. In my mind, there was no point of finishing the bar exam because I would receive failing scores for every section up to that point. When my test booklet was collected, I hurried outside of the testing area not knowing what I would do next, give up or persevere.

Perseverance

Being determined to achieve and perseverance go hand and hand. You cannot have one without the other. Perseverance is telling yourself to get the job done no matter what. If this were a Nike ad, I would say, "Just do it." But in all seriousness, that is exactly what perseverance requires, attitude plus action.

If I were to ask you to define perseverance in your own words, you would probably use one or a combination of the following words and phrases: overcoming, persistence, resolute, never giving up, resolve, resilience, determination, steadfast, and endurance. You might even use stubbornness. What is often overlooked when defining perseverance is what happens prior to the action taking place; the person persevering makes a conscious decision to keep going, keep fighting, and not give up. Not only is that what I did during the Tennessee Bar Exam, but you too must make the same conscious decision to keep fighting until you get the desired result.

For the first few minutes outside of the testing area, I paced back and forth not knowing where to go or what I was going to do next. My laptop crashing left me completely discombobulated. Eventually, I walked upstairs in the auditorium and ended up sitting in an opening that led to seating above the testing area. Sometime between my frantic pacing and walking upstairs, I picked up my cell phone and car keys from the check-in counter. Although I was sitting down at this point, the keys to my car were still in my hand. I thought to myself; I might as well leave because there is no way I can come back from this. I even reasoned I could simply re-take the examination in five months when it was offered again.

As I began to grip my keys tighter, I decided to text a few people before I made my exit. I informed them of how disastrous the first half of testing had gone. Most of the people I sent text messages further contributed to my temporary state of ridiculousness and pity. However, a couple texted back telling me something I already knew; I drove all the way there, and I might as well finish the exam. Despite the text messages not being the most encouraging, it was exactly what I needed to hear. Honestly, I was not ready to throw in the towel nor was I willing. I had thirty more minutes before the second half of testing began. That was all the time I needed to come to my senses, gain my composure, and focus like never before. I made up my mind to persevere.

O. A. O. T. S. G.

The subtitle of this book is unleashing your greatness, and there is no better time to unleash it than when obstacles become apparent. Hence, the heading of this section, O. A. O. T. S. G. stands for obstacles are opportunities to show greatness. You must use whatever obstacle or hindrance in your path to success as a stepping-stone to elevate yourself to greater heights. Show the world that you are resilient. Show the world that you are an overcomer. Show the world what you are born with. Show the world your greatness.

At the conclusion of the break, it was time to enter the testing area and answer the last six essays of the day. When I sat down in my assigned seat, the tech supervisor brought my laptop to me and stated that I was free to use it on the last six essays. There was a brief moment of relief; then reality struck again. Passing this bar exam would be more difficult than I expected going in, as there was no doubt I scored poorly in the first half of testing for day one. Before I opened the test booklet, I said a quick prayer and gave myself a quick pep talk that went something like this: "Let's go Smiley! You can do this. You will get through this. You are ready for whatever obstacle that comes your way; this is just another one. You got this!"

I did not hear anything after the pep talk other than the magic words spoken by the head proctor, "You may begin." Of course, I complied. When I looked up for what I believe to be the first time to check the clock, only a few minutes remained. I worked until the time was called. I let out a deep sigh. Testing day one was over and day two would begin early the next morning. They collected the testing materials again, and I gathered my things and went to my hotel.

Once I reached my hotel room, I had ample time to think about what had occurred. However, at that point, I was able to push it to the back of my mind and focus on the task at hand, treating this obstacle as a stepping-stone. I studied as if nothing had occurred earlier in the day. I went to sleep with one thing on my mind, excelling on day two of the bar exam. I woke up rejuvenated. It was time to finish out strong.

I followed the same procedures as the day before. When I got to my seat, several of the other bar takers approached me commending me on keeping my cool during my computer meltdown, but if they only knew. One woman, in particular, approached me and said she had the same experience when she was sitting for the New York Bar Exam. She told me she passed that examination, and she was confident I would pass. Although it was a nice comment, it seemed odd; she did not know me or anything about my ability to comprehend legal concepts, but I thanked her nonetheless. Not long after, it was time to begin day two of testing. Day two went by quickly.

That night I did nothing related to the bar exam, except look up the date results would be released. The results were going to be released on April 8th by 2 p.m., which was over a month away. While waiting for the results, I had plenty of time to reflect back on how I became more focused after my laptop crashed. I realized that I did not need my laptop to succeed, nor did I need any extrinsic item because I was born with everything I needed to excel and exceed expectations, and it was up to me to unleash it.

On Friday, April 8th, 2016, I went to my office and pulled up the website where the results would be uploaded for the world to see. The results were not up yet. I eventually became distracted and consumed with my work. My computer screen blinked and I directed my eyes toward it. I saw a list of several names. My name was amongst the list of successful applicants.

Don't Stop Now

Being determined to achieve is not a narrow concept or mentality, nor should it be limited to one area of your life. Being determined is a lifestyle, which includes the concepts of perseverance, conscious decision-making, and the attitude that you can accomplish all things. Whether you make a conscious decision to take on a task or it is thrust upon you, adopting this lifestyle will cause you not only to achieve but also to excel. Once you begin to achieve and show the world your greatness, do not stop. Make the most of your gifts, and become the best version of yourself. The only limits are those that you place on yourself.

Some time, after I received the good news about my Tennessee Bar passage, I went to the barbershop. I was there to get a haircut, but like most guys who frequent a barbershop, I began conversing about everything from sports to life. Usually, the conversations are pretty general. This time was different. My barber told me that he saw my Facebook post about my recent bar passage. He congratulated me, but he did not stop there. He told me I was an inspiration to him and to everyone else trying to

142

make their dreams a reality. Honestly, people have said that before, but I have never really engaged the individual who made the statement in an in-depth conversation. But this was different because my barber was a young business owner and I was at the barbershop, so of course, I continued the conversation.

During our conversation, he made a comment that I gave more thought than anything else we discussed that day. He said, "Keep your foot on the gas." I nodded my head and said, "No doubt." I did not need him to explain what he meant because at that moment it was clear. After I had finished getting a haircut, I got in the car and headed home. I did not turn on the radio; I just thought about what my barber said. It was profound.

Keeping your foot on the gas means continued effort toward achieving your goal. It means setting new goals and approaching those goals with the same vigor and energy, more if necessary, as the goals you have already accomplished. It means constant, never-ending pursuit of discovering, utilizing, and unleashing your inherent power, which allows you to show the world your greatness. It means not only seeing the bigger picture but being proactive to bring it to fruition. It means achieving against all odds. It means taking steps toward the fulfillment of your purpose when you are alone on the journey, and the road is not straight, and the path is not clear. So my advice to you is keep your foot on the gas in spite of your circumstances, good or bad.

Southern Baptist preachers have a saying when they are getting ready to conclude their sermon. I will follow their lead. "I am getting ready to close." But, before I do let me leave you with a poem by Mr. William Ernest Henley, titled "Invictus," which means unconquerable or unsubdued.

> Out of the night that covers me,
> Black as the Pit from pole to pole,
> I thank whatever gods may be
> For my unconquerable soul.
>
> In the fell clutch of circumstance
> I have not winced nor cried aloud.
> Under the bludgeonings of chance
> My head is bloody, but unbowed.
>
> Beyond this place of wrath and tears
> Looms but the Horror of the shade,
> And yet the menace of the years
> Finds, and shall find, me unafraid.
>
> It matters not how strait the gate,
> How charged with punishments the scroll,
> I am the master of my fate:
> I am the captain of my soul.

"Invictus" embodies what it means to be determined to achieve. Mr. Henley was speaking directly to you and I. I heard him loud and clear. Did you? My mindset and approach to life are forever changed. The only thing that can stop me is death. If I am living, I cannot see any reason I Can Not![51] Can you?

---

[51] I am well aware that this is not grammatically correct.

CONCLUSION

There is no better way to end this book than by discussing where it all began. For centuries, people have attempted to say certain sects of the population were better than others. Those individuals have tried to use various platforms to justify their deeply held beliefs. Nevertheless, all platforms speak to a beginning point, in which all (wo)men are derived. In the words of Dr. Martin Luther King Jr. "All men are created equal." All men are born with an untapped potential for greatness.

For me, I discovered my inherent power through trial and error and from paying particular attention to those around me. I learned from everyone I encountered, from my mother and father to those individuals who were only in my life for a season. It took time, but I was able to discover, utilize, and maximize my inherent power.

In August of 2012, I began a journey that would change my life; not only did my life change but my perspective as well. I moved into low incoming housing in a high crime area of North Little Rock, Arkansas. I did not have a job nor did I receive any significant financial support from family. All I had was a goal and well wishes of my loved ones, and I am sure some of them doubted. Although my circumstances seemed bleak, the end goal was my only thought—becoming JB Smiley Jr., Esq. On September 8, 2015, which was my birthday, my end goal became my reality; I became JB Smiley Jr., Esq.

I recognize that my journey is not over, but it is an ongoing process. The most meaningful thing I have learned on my journey thus far is that the essential attributes and characteristics are those that are innate and common to us all. Whether you properly develop, utilize, and maximize those innate attributes and characteristics is up to you. They are vital to your short-term and long-term success. You will not be able to unleash your greatness without doing so. Be proactive! Be intentional! Make the most of your inherent power.

They say hindsight is 20/20, and that saying holds true. When I look back, properly developing my inherent power, setting goals, making sacrifices, being disciplined and determined to achieve my goals were well worth it, and it will be for you as well. Know what you want, focus on what you want, and be determined to achieve it. Unleash your greatness!

Best wishes,

JB Smiley Jr.

www.ingramcontent.com/pod-product-compliance
Lightning Source LLC
LaVergne TN
LVHW011332080426
835513LV00006B/309